D0514467

'[Dean's] grandfather, Heinz Schapira, was a Jewish refugee from the Nazis, sent away as a teenager with his brother just before the outbreak of the Second World War. And Heinz's father, David, had himself been a refugee from Ukraine in the previous war . . . **Their stories are extraordinary . . . An admirably humane and curious book**' Steven Poole, *Guardian*

'**An extraordinary family tale of survival and perseverance over two generations.** Jonathan Dean's remarkable family saga would make the producers of *Who Do You Think You Are?* weak at the knees . . . His great-grandfather David, Dean recounts, was blinded by Italian mortar shrapnel in 1917 and, before being shipped off to a concentration camp, suffered the agony of having to say goodbye to his sons at Vienna's railway station. No less harrowing are the stories of war and leaking vessels on the Mediterranean told by today's refugees whom Dean encounters along the way'

Tarquin Hall, *Sunday Times*

'A mix of family history, travel memoir and meditation on today's political climate. David [Dean's great-grandfather] fought in the First World War, fled anti-Semitism in Ukraine and moved to Vienna, where he became a lawyer. After Nazi Germany annexed Austria in 1938, David and his wife Tina sent their teenage sons Heinz and Rudi to England through the Kindertransport network . . . **Dean's writing is winning. He explores complex subjects accessibly, and his book is all the more powerful for it**' Max Liu, *i Newspaper*

Jonathan Dean is Senior Writer for the *Sunday Times* Culture, regularly interviewing the world's biggest stars. He has also written for the paper's News Review, Style, Magazine and Travel sections, on subjects ranging from Remembrance Day to holidays in LA, and contributed to the *Pool, GQ, Shortlist,* the *Independent* and *Red.*

I MUST BELONG
SOMEWHERE

Jonathan Dean

WEIDENFELD & NICOLSON

First published in Great Britain in 2017
by Weidenfeld & Nicolson.
This paperback edition published in 2018
by Weidenfeld & Nicolson
an imprint of the Orion Publishing Group Ltd
Carmelite House, 50 Victoria Embankment
London EC4Y 0DZ

An Hachette UK Company

1 3 5 7 9 10 8 6 4 2

ISBN (Mass Market Paperback) 978 1 4746 0448 2
ISBN (eBook) 978 1 4746 0449 9

Typeset by Input Data Services Ltd, Somerset

Printed and bound by CPI Group (UK) Ltd, Croydon, CR0 4YY

www.orionbooks.co.uk

To family past, present and future

Chapter 1

I stayed up late with my grandfather's wartime diaries on the first night, feeling closer to him and my past than ever before. An Austrian refugee in Britain, writing in his mother tongue before his English improved, it was like sitting next to foreigners on the tube who are talking about pop music as, sometimes, there were a few names I recognised peeking through. Always places, like Hyde Park, Norwood and Brighton. He included photos of London's chimney pots in moonlight and a list of the films he saw. He enjoyed *The Hunchback of Notre Dame*. He reveals his favourite books as well, and one was called *The Jewish Problem*. He calls music hall 'feeble entertainment' and that is something I nod along to. I mean, it is, isn't it?

* * *

The cathedral square in the centre of Cologne is packed with dozens of tourist groups, mostly from Japan. They walk in pairs taking pictures of what they are told to notice. It's a big public space of very little design or buzz and it's dirty too; right next to a vast central station with a glass roof smeared opaque through time, steam and oil. Cologne is, I think, as I walk around it, a little like a rubbish Vienna, but for my grandfather Heinz Israel Schapira – on a stopover during his journey to London just before the Second World War broke out – Vienna, the city he had fled, was long gone. This new and inferior one was a step to sanctuary that must have felt like an embrace. He arrived in Cologne from Frankfurt at 4 a.m. on 8 August 1939. He writes in his diaries that he laughed with fellow refugees who had travelled from all over Nazi Europe. These teenagers, taking different onward routes to Britain, were yelling to each other on the streets. Gasps like: 'See you in Bloomsbury House!' And Heinz writes of this changeover, like a schoolboy does of a trip to the zoo; enthusiastic and informative. His older brother, Rudi, and a family friend, Mary, 'wander cheerfully' through the town. It was pitch black in that eeriest and most imaginative time of night; in pre-dawn, when yesterday is already memory and tomorrow is making plans.

'Not a soul, neither pedestrian or policeman, just a few cars,' writes Heinz. 'Milkmen, road sweepers . . . When it is light, we sit in a park, dreadfully tired, but feeling great.'

I took to those same Cologne streets decades later – early in the autumn of 2015. I was over in the city for work, to interview the actor Christian Slater, but the work was short and so, afterwards, I had time to myself, to amble and walk across an old bridge by the station with those ubiquitous European padlocks, clipped by lovers onto wire fences with initials in marker pen. It was a dreary day, sky blended into concrete buildings, and the padlocks only sparkled when the sun broke briefly, illuminating the names of couples probably long since unchained.

In his diary, Heinz says of Mary, 'She is wonderful!' They would kiss the day after they left Cologne, after taking a train on which they drank some wine – which is remarkably similar to how I started dating my wife. Perhaps these stomach pangs of love are why my grandfather wrote, in Cologne, of being 'noticed because of our high spirits . . . others call me a "travelling salesman in shirt sleeves"'. I do not know why, rushing around Nazi Germany, one month before the war broke out, the young Jewish trio weren't scared, terrified, hiding. Or, at least, quiet. But they have all gone now, so it's something I will never know. I think they were probably just young and giddy.

Three months after I was in Cologne, there were over a thousand complaints of assault made by women during and after a New Year's Eve parade. Most of the assaults were sexual and led to the arrest of many asylum seekers and migrants, and the inevitable, subsequent revenge attacks on people who were not white, which led to the usual increase in fascist and counter-fascist marching. While I was there, however, everything looked more assimilated. This glimpse of societal sobriety I should have dismissed as helplessly naive. But you see what you want to see and, to my eyes, it was all types of people meshed. A Turkish man pushed a cleaning cart. Another strode with purpose wearing a suit. Men of African origin played 'Stand by Me' on banjo and guitar.

That traditional, awful harmonica that drones through all German tourist spots, played by one old man who looked like his family had been local for generations, and another, younger, who seemed Balkan. I passed a betting shop full of desperate white men and desperate black men, who all needed money, and were putting the livelihood of their families into guesswork about horses. Two things were clear. One, many of these people who appear foreign may not think of themselves as foreign any more. Two, their children certainly won't.

My night in Cologne coincided with Germany's huge intake of refugees from Syria who, if the news was to be believed, were overwhelming the train network in carriages built for half the number they suddenly needed to hold. Herded like cattle through safe, regimented Europe. Down on the ground, I didn't see this. It felt normal, serene at the station, where I spotted commuters of all races, neatness, styles; refugees from a decade passed – or the day just gone – already blended in the background of their new, occasionally welcoming, home. Wallpaper, really, is what they had become.

But what happened on New Year's Eve muddled this, confused and shook people. People who felt content in their politics now had to think about things a little more deeply, address a really twitchy and layered issue. First, those who always welcomed refugees felt uneasy. Secondly, those who did not welcome them started to worry about how far politics may lean to the right if they became even more unwelcoming and vocal. What is the acceptable limit of the right? A third lot, who didn't really think in the first place, just fought on the internet and streets, and it was a political, social, sensitive mess – a shambolic painting of the continent created by clenched fists.

That summer, I think, Europe changed. It no longer felt as easy and fun as it did when I was growing up; when the greatest concern of anyone I knew was how to fit its wonders into an InterRail pass.

As I left the station in Cologne I spotted a café built into its outside wall. Heinz found one too, he writes in his diaries, and with so much journey, mystery and Mary on its way, he ordered a black coffee as a pick me up. The café that I see is Dean & David and so I order a black coffee too. I enjoy bookends and match-ups, cute and coincidental, and I note the name of the café uses both my surname, and the first name of my great-grandfather: Heinz's father, David Schapira. He was also a refugee (not to mention a widower, blind man, singer, lawyer, concentration camp survivor, memoir-writer, soldier). The name of that café in Cologne is nothing more than chance, but it's nice all the same.

It was another morning and they were talking about refugees on the radio. Month umpteen of the crisis, and numbers were rising. So much bad news that won't go away and it was impossible to think of a time when it wasn't there; it had become almost normal now and, like sheet rain all summer long, you wished you could do something, but knew you were powerless. You live in a country that's only taking a handful of Syrians and such and so it's best just to donate a sum and shake your head, go to work feeling lucky and looking sad.

So went the summer of 2015, the least silly of silly seasons. (At least until the following year.) Every single night on the news, rows and rows of people moving slowly through Europe and then – when the season chilled to autumn and winter – the one change was that these people walked through mud and snow. Their clothes stayed the same. Thinly lined jackets and short-sleeved shirts; Premier League football tops and baseball caps. The same whether in the height of summer on a stuffy Hungarian plain, or sinking into a ditch behind a barrier at the Serbian border when the rest of us were planning Christmas. I noticed these details when our nights turned cold. The battle to keep the heating off as long as you can. Maybe, if we have an extra layer, we can last until November . . . But these people owned one set of clothes, and nothing shows somebody has fled their home in a hurry, to travel across all sorts of heat and terrain for a time they know, but won't admit, is forever, more than wearing the same clothes and shoes.

I am very lucky. I have led a life of safety and decent success, crammed with love. I am happy. I am grateful. I am a white, straight, British, middle-class male so everything could be catastrophically worse and yet, I never really thought how. How I made it to here. Nobody does. The past is the past and my summer of 2015 was spent staying with various friends and my family while the house my wife and I had bought in a decent area of London had its new kitchen fitted. Our baby turned one and he spent his days playing with a bright wooden train set that was a gift from a thought-ful aunt. He spilt food all over himself so we changed his clothes. My wife, Rosamund, readied herself to head back to a job on a lifestyle magazine following an entire year of maternity leave, while we went to three excellent music festivals and planned what carpets to buy for the upstairs. We followed the news. Of course we did. Apart from anything else, working on a news-paper, that's sort of my job. On the radio, television and the internet; all the ways people do now, when it's become impossible to ignore. We read in-depth articles about the plight of people who were incalculably worse off than us, probably dead by the time we reached the final paragraph, but our lives needed leading and – as everyone does – we honed in our own concerns. They were so minor, but they mattered to us. Our baby went through a tough first fortnight at nursery and it's hard to think beyond him, even to the body of a boy washed up on the beach. When you pick your baby up after spending the whole day worrying about him at work, and he smells differently to how he used to and he starts to cry, he is everything.

Then, somebody on the radio mentioned Kindertransport.

Kindertransport means Children's Transport and the person was mooting that Britain should do as it did between 1938 and 1940; bring thousands of young refugees to our relatively safe shores. Back then, it was due to the Nazis and the kids were German or Austrian. Or from further east. Today it's Isis, or Assad, and the kids are largely from Syria: a combination of woe in an endless war very far away. It is fair to be upset and then do nothing. I do. We all do, pretty much, or else all our money would be in charities and our spare rooms filled with sad strangers. But, despite this, there was a jolt when I heard Kindertransport, like a time that you hear the name of an ex who you hurt, or see their photo. A name and a reminder that picks you up and places you somewhere else.

I knew more about Brad Pitt than my grandfather Heinz and his brother Rudi but I did know that, as Jews, they fled Austria as teenagers. It was in 1939, which means they must, or could have been on Kindertransport, or something similar, and this is the very simplest thinking in the discipline of determinist philosophy, but because somebody helped Heinz – aged sixteen – flee an oppressive regime seventy-five years ago, I was able to sit in a brand new kitchen in London, listen to the *Today* programme and hear about a politician's plan to bring back Kindertransport.

The Kindertransport rescue trips took place in the nine months leading up to the outbreak of the Second World War. All told, around ten thousand children – mostly Jews – made the journey to the United Kingdom. And, mostly, they would never see their families again. The initiative was set up after word spread internationally of what happened on Kristallnacht, 9 and 10 November 1938, when evenings were spent wilfully destroying Jewish businesses throughout fascist Europe.

Broken glass and smashed synagogues gave the horror its crystal name and it sounds festive, glittering, too pretty for a night that took the lives of nearly one hundred Jews and led a further thirty thousand to concentration camps. Over seven thousand businesses were destroyed, and it didn't stop at dawn. Weeks later, in the Sachsenhausen concentration camp, sixty-two Jews were beaten for so long and hard that some policemen apparently had to turn their backs lest they saw.

When protestors gathered in London in 2015, with placards that challenged the government to accommodate more Syrian refugees, many home-painted pieces of card had a line from a poem by the Somalian Warsan Shire.

No one leaves home unless home is the mouth of a shark. You only run for the border when you see the whole city running as well.

After the tumult of Kristallnacht, some of the Jews taken from their family homes and flung into distant captivity had their eyes knocked out and their faces flattened so they held no shape. A Google Image search for 'Syria Atrocities' will tell you more of what happened there to prompt its citizens to leave than I could explain here.

This mention of Kindertransport had suddenly turned a political crisis very personal indeed and even if, later, I discovered that Heinz's train wasn't officially under that name and government banner – that his father instead had to secure passes called Trainee Permits – it's all the same. My grandfather was a refugee who came from Vienna to London on a train, and I knew so little about how his history was even possible, let alone what it was like for him when he came to the country that is my home. Heinz, you see, died when I was five, in 1985, and he has always been a name rather than a body to me. I remember him very fondly if vaguely. A little like the film *E.T.* I know it's good, that it made me happy and that the ending was sad, but I can't quite remember why.

It's lucky, then, that my grandfather kept diaries. Extensive diaries, stored in two bulky ring-binders – one purple, one black – of hundreds and hundreds of pages of words, tables, documents and newspaper cuttings. The diaries are an account of a man in a strange country, day-by-day detail of being a refugee in England and all the hate, hope and drizzle that brings. They have been in my house for a long time, brought over by my mum, Anne, a few years ago like some sort of heritage baton, but left unread. Magazines piled on top of them. Tea spilt over the early chapters. A spider's web spun in the metal claw that holds the hole-punched pages. Much is covered in dust, which looked liked neglect, so I started reading them last summer.

It was simple. There was a refugee crisis and my grandfather was a refugee and wrote about it. It felt a bit weird to not read them.

I began to take it in – this family history that is not so much secret as ignored. My attention span jerks like a cricket's head, regardless of how into something I am. This is the privilege of a comfortable millennial. A brain never forced to focus on one task too hard, that is allowed to wander and look for entertainment. But, out the back of my house, in a nothing stretch of hall between the stairs and the downstairs toilet, where my computer is set up, where little distracts me other than the whir of the boiler and snails creeping up a pile of bricks by a glass back door, I settled down to read.

It was slow-going. Mainly as the diaries start in German, but later, with the pages in English, reading them only made me realise where my terrible handwriting comes from. Heinz was writing thousands of words each day, tired and confused, sometimes resting paper on his leg at the foot of a hard wooden bed. I flicked, trying to settle on something, and the first page that I read in full, when he had been in his new country for a while, in the second volume, had him writing that he didn't know if he would 'ever be able to find a woman in this country completely likeable . . . They are absolutely crazy.' He ended up marrying two.

It's the beginning, though, that is so timely when the diaries open with a document whose introductory line reads: 'Der Jude Heinz Israel Schapira'. A swastika is stamped on the bottom left and it feels like the last scene from *Cabaret*, when evil started to linger at the front of the stage.

My grandfather had a serial number – 17970 – that marked him a prisoner and a date – 24 July 1939 – that feels like a best before.

Next is a document listing the luggage he took on the train from Vienna to London, via Frankfurt and Cologne. There is a shirt, books, chess set, pyjamas, a towel, a pair of scissors and – which must have been a 1930s thing – a hairnet. All loud echoes of people travelling across Europe now, in clothes that never change. Whether in a suitcase, rucksack, bag or pocket, refugees from my grandfather's time or today take so few personal effects with them that, even if we are told it's better to cherish memories than possessions, I wonder what choice such people have. If their memories are nightmares and possessions something they used to have, I don't know if there's anything to cling to.

Heinz writes of what it is like to leave home, and the more I read, more and more headlines scream about how Europe is shutting up shop. Hungary closing its borders to Serbia, a main route for Syrian refugees. My attention flips from iPhone to old diary page, back and forth again, again. As Heinz, Rudi and Mary near the Dutch border, a customs official starts intimidating them. Between Serbia and Hungary, desperate people are put in makeshift jails, before being sent back to where they're from, or somewhere else, where they're not from. Where do they go? In his diary, my grandfather writes of how he was sneered at by a customs official, told he would be strip-searched by that bully, that he, Rudi and Mary would never make it as far as London. Three teenagers on a train taking them from a place that would end up killing most people they know, being told that they would never make it to the place they were going. They would have to go back. When Heinz and his party were told they wouldn't make it, it must have felt like a door slamming. He and his travel companions sat still in the carriage. They offered the guard money as that must have felt like the only thing to do. They offered bribes and the guard paced, laughing, bellowing insults and threats under no authority than his own twisted sense of humour. Seconds stretched into hours and when the guard relented, as he had no reason to make them stay in Germany and probably couldn't face the paperwork, Heinz could finally feel free. The guard doesn't even take the money. Heinz buys aftershave and chocolate instead.

It was this moment, I guess, when my grandfather crossed that border, which puts me here. The key switch from a past with no future to a future that would allow his descendants to be blasé about the past. Of the moment the train pulled from Germany into The Netherlands, Heinz wrote: 'Border! Holland! Blue-white-red flags! Freedom!!! A wonderful feeling!' . . . In the news, every day, in a sentence with no risk of becoming dated, hordes of migrants sit stranded behind razor-wire fence and I google 'learn from history' to see if we ever learn anything from history. I come across George Bernard Shaw's quote, 'We learn from history that we learn nothing from history.'

It's the humanity that chokes with the first look at my grandfather's diaries, a glimpse of light in the darkest conditions: a flower on a battlefield. Humour and humanity; every overused metaphor that writers – or Terrence Malick – uses in the struggle to talk about war. It was there, on the journey to England. He is impressed by a dining car ('Wonderfully soft, clean, comfortable, bright'); less so Holland ('. . . dreadfully monotonous and flat . . . Unfortunately few windmills'); and on the journey from Vienna to London seems to be flirting with Mary ('. . . cuddling, chatting, getting to know each other better: a great girl!'). Once on the boat across the sea – 'My very first sea voyage!' – they share a cigarette. Of a view, Heinz writes, 'It is beautiful; sunshine, sea as flat as a mirror, seagulls, not a trace of seasickness! The greatest adventure! We soon find seats in the sun and sit there with our eyes closed.' Earlier, on the train, excited, seeing the whole ordeal as a big adventure, the trio didn't seem terrified but rather lark about speaking the English they know, which consists of the description 'posh and laughing'; actually a fair two words for how my grandfather's eventual English family would be.

When they arrive at the coast, Heinz writes, 'Should we kiss the ground, cry? No, we are too tired for any bursts of sentiment!' Then, on the train from the port of Harwich to London they are invited to dinner in the dining car by an English lady. 'What do you do with 3 spoons, 4 knives and 5 forks?' asks Heinz, bewildered. He and I have that sort of confusion in common. Then, after forty hours of travelling, they pull into Liverpool Street. That we have in common too, because it is the station I use most days.

After fourteen minutes my train pulls into Liverpool Street from Walthamstow, where I live, via St James Street, Clapton, Hackney Downs and Bethnal Green – the ever-changing neighbourhoods of east London that I came to know and love during my twenties and early thirties, in parks and pubs and the couches of friends. Usually, I travel during rush hour and the train is packed, with elbows in faces and forehead sweat even on a frozen morning. Milky coffee spilt from polystyrene cups onto white trainers. It's crammed from eight, when I usually travel, speeding at various slow speeds, very rarely getting a seat, mostly standing, trying to read a book with one hand, or browsing the news on my phone while listening to an album I've heard is cool. Such is the routine of my nice life, in which, for under quarter of an hour, most days, I am cramped. Past nine, the train is empty enough for a seat and, from ten, it's emptied so much that whole sets of seats are free to flout the rules and rest my feet on. So, as the train travels past the marshes and empty warehouses on the periphery of heavily populated Hackney, over green spaces and fishing lakes, I think, there is a lot of room here. So much space. So much available land so close to London's bull's-eye and yet we hear people all the time, interviewed in big suburban gardens near ornate fish ponds, who think this country is too crowded. Where, they say, as a second gin hits, would we fit the refugees? How can we possibly take any more of them?

It used to be hard to find anyone with such vocal opinions. But they became such a tabloid movement that political parties were founded for their benefit which, in turn, forced the more mainstream parties these people used to vote for to move to the right and try to win them back. And so, now, the idea Britain is full is no longer a shamefully racist thing, but rather a genuine fear that job security is under threat if thousands of foreigners come into the country and look for and find work. Therefore people say there is no more room, say that about anybody; foreign and economic migrants and terrified refugees are lumped into the same non-British pot, railed at by people whose job prospects have been slashed due to our stringent economic circumstances. Scapegoated. But it takes a bit too long to explain boom and bust cycles and how an ageing population causes strain on the NHS and various other public expenditure issues, so opportunistic politicians pander to this race card instead, creating divisions and amping up the fear of foreigners. Deflection, the oldest political trick, summarised here as, 'How could we possibly fit any more in?'

Well, how about here? Here in the wide open spaces of the route which my grandfather once took, into one of the world's busiest cities, which still has gaps to fill. How about there? Four tower blocks twenty storeys high to house six thousand refugees. I don't understand people who care more about the green belt and a field or space for a shed, than the lives of fellow and innocent humans, but they seem to make up at least half of this country. And I know that it is far more complicated than building homes, because the tougher issue is the provision of jobs and services, but that is rarely the first argument of the person who is resolutely anti-immigration and anti-refugee. Their first argument refers to space and, so, they would not have allowed my grandfather in.

After all, his generation of refugees was not welcomed by everyone. 'The way stateless Jews from Germany are pouring in from every port of this country is becoming an outrage' ran an extreme newspaper story in 1938. Such people would have argued Heinz wouldn't fit in this country.

From Harwich to London, then, my grandfather was on a longer version of the route that I take most days, fleeing a home country that wanted to kill him. At Liverpool Street station today, there are two statues in honour of the Kindertransport and other refugee transports that arrived in the city.

The bigger one sits outside, in a place called Hope Square, which sounds like it should be in Disneyland, carved into the shape of five children with their suitcases waiting quietly at the end of a brass track. Their wide eyes look anywhere but back, a girl holds a teddy bear and a boy sits with a violin case by his feet. A line from the Talmud says: 'Whosoever rescues a single soul is credited as though they had saved the whole world.' I note, on a visit one wet Tuesday morning, that the sculptor was Frank Meisler and that he was a child saved by the Kindertransport. A big plaque on the station wall is inscribed: 'Children of the Kindertransport: Who found hope and safety in Britain through the gateway of Liverpool Street Station . . . In gratitude to the people of Britain for saving the lives of 10,000 unaccompanied mainly Jewish children who fled from Nazi persecution in 1938 and 1939.'

That's only 10,000. At least 1.5 million Jewish children died in the Holocaust. It's meagre, but meagre is better than nothing.

I watch commuters walk by the statue and commemorative words, glued to phones, possibly reading about the migrant crisis, on a left- or right-wing news site. Probably looking at Instagram. What nearly everyone thinks has set in by their mid twenties and I wonder if anybody ever has their mind changed by anything they read on the internet these days; a continuous affirmation of a belief system on media channels of choice. A huge man in a bold electric-blue suit, loose trousers soaking up the rain, stands in front of the plaque. His back is turned to another man with his hood up, staring at the condensation patterns on passing bus windows.

They are both smoking, standing still, and when I walk towards them they walk away. I was going to ask what they know about Hope Square, what those words on the statue mean. But before I can, the man in the hood has gone, leaving the other temporarily exposed before he looks down, has a very long drag and disappears into the crowds. I don't ask either of them anything in the end, but that's not too much of a loss. We presume everything nowadays, our opinions based on appearance and I can't pretend I'm better. The second man was a city worker, in an aesthetically naff chain store suit, smoking at the station because he doesn't want to talk to the smokers at work. He probably just reads the free sheets, feeling sad about refugees for the length of a headline.

Who has the time for anything else?

The statue has become a big publicly funded ash-tray. Soggy cigarette butts gather behind a sign that says PRAGUE, where some of the children came from, and two empty McDonald's coffee cups sit and fill with rain. A woman in tight black jeans cradles a laptop bag under an arm and flicks ash into the nearest cup. Her umbrella covers most of her face and she is staring at nothing, certainly not the five bronze children right in front of her, not even the grim, grey London sky, as dull as slate. She's a smoker, though, like everyone else on Hope Square, and many smokers smoke in order to be left alone, lost in thoughts about nothing.

The second statue is smaller, by the ticket machines on the mainline platform concourse, above the tube entrance and under a big Meeting Point sign. It has two children on it, a boy and a girl and, at the top of its low plinth, under a tossed Burger King wrapper and scattered fries, I read its shoe-scuffed sign. 'Für Das Kind – Displaced', with an extra line, 'Celebrating The Greatness of Ordinary People in Extraordinary Times'. It lists the stations the memorial represents. One, of course, is Liverpool Street, where it stands, and the another main one is Westbahnhof, in Vienna – the second to last place where Heinz and Rudi ever saw their mother, back in 1939. I stand in the fretting atoms of commuters and *City AM* floggers, tourists who can't read ticket machines and the suited men and women powering to the City. Nobody notices either statue and, frankly, until now, neither did I. This isn't sanctimony. I assumed what a stranger thinks by the look of him. But the statues may as well not be there: as noticeable as tears in a troubled foreign country, which only reach us when they join together and form a flood.

As I turn to leave, I take in the boy on the second statue once more and spot his shoes. They look like modern trainers with Velcro. They are not from the time of the Kindertransport and I don't know what the thinking behind that was, but, for me, it brings this monument to a past rescue effort right up to date.

Children fled Nazis in brogues. Children flee Syria in Velcro trainers. Why are children still fleeing?

Where can they belong?

In 2014, there were more than 50 million refugees in the world for the first time since the Second World War. Half were – still are – children and yet more borders close, governments bicker and boys wash up on beaches. I guess, in my inaction, I was little better than people who say we shouldn't accept anyone else. That we are too crowded. Because I forgot where and who I came from. My great-grandfather David was a refugee too, fleeing the Russians in 1914, 'trying to reach the next safe haven before nightfall', he writes in his memoir, which I ask my mum for a copy of. (It arrives as a PDF.) My past, it turns out, began in an orthodox Jewish rural region of eastern Europe, before heading west to Vienna by necessity, only to have to flee again, being taken to London, where I live now; in this cosmopolitan metropolis of all sorts with backgrounds even more varied and recently far flung than my own. I forgot, maybe, because I am British and being British is easy for most. It allows you to ignore what is scary and terrible. To fuss over things that are not.

My grandfather's diaries and his father's small book make me think about all the blood that's been spilt for me. In David's memoir, he said that 'the hardest day' was when his two boys left Vienna for London. He lost his sight to shrapnel when he was nineteen, so that's some sad boast for the title of saddest day. I wonder what he would have been thinking on the first night that his sons stayed in a home far away from home. My own son, Ezra, is rarely more than a landing away from me. My ancestors, on that first night, were at 10 Windermere Avenue, north-west London, Heinz's diary details, and that's close to where I live; turn left around the North Circular, follow Google Maps. If Heinz hadn't been taken in by the family that lived there or found a farmer to give him work – 'Dung carting. Half day off. Learnt Spanish' – or moved to Reading – 'Very miserable evening in rainy Reading' – or survived an attack by a bull on 26 July 1940, I wouldn't be here. And, again, this is very basic thinking and it doesn't make me at all special, but as thousands like my grandfather try to escape exactly the dangers that he escaped, I wonder why this modern crisis didn't resonate earlier.

Perhaps it's because Syria is further away. The Nazis were just . . . there. The Middle East is over . . . there. Wars have been fought in that part of the world for decades now and, after so many, it's hard to tell them apart. But, relatively speaking, we British, as I write, are taking very few Syrians in and they are – like my grandfather had been – in danger of their lives if they don't get help.

It's messed up. They must belong somewhere. Like I do, here. Here because someone allowed Heinz in on a trainee permit, whatever that is, and he stayed and met my English grandmother and became very English himself, and then the rest happened. We are all our own jigsaw, I suppose, and it feels wrong to dismiss the chance every other human should be given to start piecing together their own, like I have mine. I know it's hard, but it's harder for the ones you are being hard on.

When I was younger, in my late teens, when no decision is thought through, I decided to do a philosophy degree. I was faced with a UCAS form and worried parents and fussy teachers demanding I made plans. My final choice was of little comfort to them, as job prospects for philosophy graduates usually involve the words 'freelance' and 'drugs', but other people, from that summer on, did seem impressed by my choice of study. The subject sounds taxing and intelligent and outsiders don't really know what students of philosophy actually do, which creates mystique around a three-year course which is often little more than sitting in some seminar asking each other if the statement, 'This is a lie' is, in fact, a lie. The work, mostly, isn't relevant. Most of it is just mad.

What I do remember, though, were the lectures we had on determinism. This, for example, is from the website ˙ The Information Philosopher: 'Determinism is the philosophical idea that every event or state of affairs, including every human decision and action, is the inevitable and necessary consequence of antecedent states of affairs.' Or as really ancient Greek philosopher Leucippus put it, 'Nothing occurs at random, but everything for a reason and by necessity.'

There is, in other words, no room for chance. This you learn early on in a philosophy degree – perhaps to comfort those who suddenly realised they were wasting their time and other people's money by being there.

I would talk about determinism in the student union and while others lined up shots I lined up matches in a row on booze-sticky tables to explain that each match was an event and how one match necessarily leads on to another. My audience would dwindle, but I would carry on and explain one match could represent an event seventeen years ago, something that has stuck. An early, forming memory, say, of a good friend with a broken arm in a big white cast. Another could be from two seconds ago. Some sharp remark that a lover made, something about them you didn't know but then struggle to forget. Either way, add them together, and the matches line up next to one another, over-and-over, to lead to whatever you are doing right now.

And, now, I am writing about my family's written history. There has always been a part of me that wanted people to know of my past, however little I knew of it myself. I thought, at my most glib, it made me more interesting. Something to add in small print on an ethnicity form, after a tick next to White British. Appropriation of a race or religion or culture that isn't your own is cheap, especially when the people you are appropriating have struggled. There is an entire episode of *Seinfeld* about Jerry's dentist Tim, who converts to Judaism and starts making victimhood Jewish jokes within the first few hours. Jerry – a Jew – is angry. You earn this stuff, you don't assume it, and yet, I did wish people knew my background, how I am more than just from Surrey.

Once, on a plane back from Los Angeles, where I often go for work, I started talking to a man sitting next to me. Bloody Mary each and we'd seen all the good films. Tall, slim, bald; he was keeping one eye on his family of four sitting across the aisle.

'So, are you from London?' he asked.

'Yes,' I said. 'Is this your first time?'

'No, I've been a lot. But my family . . . It's their first time. We're going for three days and then we're going to Cape Town.'

There was a lull in our conversation.

'It's frustrating,' continued the man. I never did ask his name. 'We were supposed to go to Tel Aviv for my son's bar mitzvah.'

(It was another month of escalated violence between Israel and Gaza.)

'That's a shame,' I replied.

'Yes. It would have been special.'

The conversation lasted no more than ten minutes, but as I sat there trying to sleep, I thought about Tel Aviv, where he said he originally planned to go. As a city, it sprawled in the late 1940s when the State of Israel was formed and communities of refugees arrived from Europe. It is somewhere that must be filled with family of mine, where David might have wanted to go if he hadn't been cattle-carted off to a concentration camp and where Heinz, I suppose, could have moved if he had not settled in England, met my grandmother, made my mother, led on to me.

And yet nobody knows any of this about me – the many matches, some burnt, some broken, some burning, some recently fizzled out, some waiting to be sparked, that led to me being me, and made a path from a distant past in a foreign country to where I am today, in London, raising a London boy with a Hebrew name, Ezra. In front of me is a gift, I thought, after reading a few pages of Heinz's diaries, and receiving David's old memoir, and I am drawn to the rest.

Many pages in, I see that Heinz wrote about good and evil and how the next generation need to overcome the work Hitler did in turning people bad. In short, his idea was that if people were once good, they can be good again. He was hopeful, which is very unlikely in a teenager whose life was already worn and lived-in. But, nowadays, there seems to be little hope again. Just last night, as I write, in another sentence that will not date, there were violent protests that turned into riots on the south coast of England.

It started off as protests against incoming migrants and refugees, from people as white and British as me. I wonder which matches line up in their past, whether any of them were foreign and forgotten. I wonder if their grandparents protested against my grandfather, who fled to this country to survive and start a British family.

Chapter 2

Soon after their sons left Austria for England in 1939, David and Tina Schapira took a trip to some friends in a town just outside Vienna. When they had last been there, their boys had been with them but now, separated by a war and an uncertain future, with just letters to keep them up to speed, Tina writes to her children that 'the swallows you saw then . . . have long since flown away, and been replaced by a new generation of birds'. During the war, letters sent from enemy territories, which Austria was, could be checked by officials for codewords. Secret messages or metaphors, heavy-handed or barely-there. There are no war secrets here. Just the words of a sad mother to a faraway part of her soul. But reading them back now, it is hard not to imagine Tina thinking of those swallows as the Jews forced to leave – or killed. And the new generation of birds as the millions now dominant, many of them filled with nationalistic hate. 'Almost all of these young swallows can already fly,' she continues. 'Only a single one's still afraid, and perches mournfully on the edge of the nest when the others fly away.' Is that one her?

*

Jutting out from the left of Vienna's Westbahnhof is an odd corrugated iron structure, which sticks up like a broken leg resting in a hospital support. The old station itself is hardly pretty – glass and stuff to hold up the glass, nothing more – but the newish metal is so ugly you can't take your eyes off it. Someone, once, thought it would be an addition so striking people would come for miles to see if it could be true. And now, they're stuck with it. I look to the right and see that, on the station's other side, that design is repeated. The planners so proud of its ostentatiousness that they made the builders build it twice. On that other side, though, it seems smaller: part-hidden by garish signs for Motel One, where rooms cost €69 per night. That not only feels like an advert for the kind of thing that happens in there, quickly, but also, robbery. From the outside, its rooms look small and, as with most stations, the area's great appeal is that it has an immediate route away from it. Massed taxi ranks and snaking trams are the image and noise; all to move people in and out.

As a key terminal in a major European city, the station found a new role to play from the summer of 2015 – that of taking refugees in and sending them off again. Behind its captivatingly daft exterior of brutal ridged metal, Motel One must, surely, have housed a great number of the grateful helpless. They arrive and are tired, or need to leave early and have no place else to go, so they head to the hotel that's nearest, that charges €69 a room, in a structure that offers some view of the city below. A capital which may, or may not, let them stay, that they may – or may not – want to be in, but which they have found themselves in anyway.

I lived in Vienna, from the age of ten to thirteen; 1991–1994. My dad, Chris, had been offered a job there by the company he worked for – IBM. The whole of eastern Europe had opened up with the drawing back of the Iron Curtain and it felt like a smart, interesting move. He worked on big projects that often involved funding from the World Bank to help kick-start the modernisation of computers in countries such as Poland, Hungary, Czech Republic and Russia. I cried when my parents told my sister Claire and me, in Pizza Hut, only finding consolation in bacon bits from the salad bar. It was a time before Stuffed Crust. I was worried mostly about my friends. I was at a comfortable preparatory school in Surrey, my life ahead inevitably leading to a comfortable secondary school in Surrey, followed by three years at one of England's top twenty universities and a job, most likely, in London, then back in Surrey. A graduate training scheme, I guess. Somewhere like Procter & Gamble, or the other one that also makes soap. Shaken from that path with a move to a foreign country I had never visited – which didn't even have a beach – I wept and said I would never make any friends again. Poor Edward and Alastair and the other ones I can't remember. Our lives were planned ahead. We would be educated, then move up the A3 to Clapham for five years, tops, marry, then back to Surrey.

One year into my life in Vienna, I never wanted to leave. There were a number of reasons. First, I was ten when I thought the move would be awful and people who are ten don't know anything. Secondly, the school I went to was mixed, and classes with girls were new to me. I found that intriguing. Thirdly, I can't overstate how fascinating the Viennese public transport system is, and I spent so much effort and time memorising its tram, bus and underground stops; the best lines to take for fun (entire U6, end of U1); which stations have the most connections that, writing this now, does make me wonder if I was a bit autistic. But, I think, actually, I was just excited. Excited to be in a city considered safe enough by my mum, Anne, for me to explore alone, bleeding that travel pass dry and counting down the days for a new line, the U3, to open. What a day that was. It opened up a quick route from our house to the tram museum.

Another reason, though, was that I never had to lose touch with things I liked back in England. Pre-email, it was long letters to Edward and Alastair. You try harder when it is harder to stay in touch. What's more, each month, family members back home would post VHS tapes and cassettes with recordings off English TV and radio. *Casualty. Don't Forget Your Toothbrush. The Archers.* A documentary here and there, usually on the Holocaust or presented by Sir David Attenborough. All the essentials, often to do with meerkats, and they helped make Vienna a home away from home. Every month, I would take the 56B bus to Hietzing to catch the U4 to Längenfeldgasse, change to the U6 to Westbahnhof and wander down to the magazine sellers in a poorly lit concourse below ground, crowds of commuters towering above me like shadows in raincoats, to buy English football and pop mags that were always old, but, to me, never out of date.

Twenty years on and the station's smarter than I remember. Brighter too, with shops that sell betterment rather than normality. Posh coffee packs and MAC cosmetics, instead of the magazines and sustenance needed for a train trip. I walk about, a meanderer crossing paths that are determined in their rush from A to B. It was here that Heinz and his brother Rudi said goodbye to their parents in 1939, my grandfather taking with him a shirt, books, chess set, pyjamas, towel, scissors and, of course, that hairnet. As the Nazis encroached, my great-grandfather David and his wife Tina tried very hard to find legal means for their sons to leave. They, eventually, secured Trainee Permits to England, but the grown-ups had to stay, afraid, perching mournfully on the edge of the nest when the others fly away.

'The hardest day for us as parents,' wrote David in the memoir he compiled in 1984, 'came on August 7th 1939, parting from our beloved boys who – because of the threat of war – were facing an uncertain future in a foreign country.'

On a good day, it takes twenty-nine minutes to travel from 14 Hohlweggasse – where the Schapira family lived in their flat – to Westbahnhof, via a quick walk and the 18 tram. That journey, that day in August, was probably taken in silence. A soon to be split family staring out of windows thinking about nothing and everything. The holding area in the station is full of steps and marble floors, smeared with the stain of constant footfall. Us people are always on the move. 10:28

to Neulengbach; 10:40 to Salzburg; 10:54 to St Polten; 10:58 to Tullnerbach-Pressbaum. Trams. Two underground lines. Buses. Taxis. Cars. So many options to leave that it is incredible anybody stays where they are, with what they are given, and doesn't leave to search for something else. Which, perversely, makes the forcing of people to move even more dehumanising. That time you don't want to go is when they actually make you go, up to a platform, to the trains that pull you away from the places and people you know, trust and love. David and Tina would have gone as far down the platform as they could, on the day their sons left, past the huts selling alcohol and snacks, so I trace footsteps as I imagine they would have fallen, and spot a franchise stall of an open sandwich shop that I liked as a boy living in the city, veering off for a moment to buy a couple of spicy egg ones.

The platform for the mainline train Heinz and Rudi took to England is behind one of many glass doors that lead to more glass doors, to a carriage door and their compartment door and eventually their seats. Each must feel like somewhere you could stop. Where you would realise there has been some mistake and that you can turn around, head back home. But the Schapiras kept walking; blind David led by quiet Tina, as close as they could to their emotional sons, everyone gripped by inner delirium.

The doors weren't automatic back then, so whoever was out in front would have reached to touch and turn the handle, knowing that walking through the opening meant another step towards goodbye. Out the front of

32

the platforms, where all the trains head, are mountains, those that surround the city. Once past them, the home on Hohlweggasse would have really felt gone. Flip your head around to the huge windows at the station's front and it's all city; the spiral of Stephansdom and much urban beauty in between. In a struggle to be named Europe's grandest capital, only Paris or Rome can possibly rival Vienna. It is, I know, a hard place to leave and the only reason that more hit songs haven't been written about Vienna is because American tourists visit France and Italy, not Austria.

Hands hold tighter when you know you have to let go. At the final door there is a turning, off to the right, which leads directly back to the sprawl of the city. No barrier. A direct line. Perhaps my grandfather would have been tempted to run, but I guess not. He was standing at the exact point where the devil and the deep blue sea is a perfectly deployed metaphor. Much had happened to force him to go, his bag packed with barely anything. It's a blank canvas of a station, Westbahnhof. Not the bustle of Penn, or the twisting adverts of Waterloo. It is a bare place for the strongest of emotions, and it's not even very big. It would have been easy to run, but if he had, he would be dead by now, most likely. Stuck on a different train that left the city to head to Poland to turn his body to ash.

Passport in hand, he boarded the train. His visa read: 'VISA FOR UNITED KINGDOM' together with the stipulations: 'GOOD FOR SINGLE JOURNEY ONLY' and 'LEAVE TO LAND GRANTED AT HARWICH THIS DAY ON CONDITION THAT THE HOLDER

WILL EMIGRATE FROM UNITED KINGDOM ON COMPLETION OF HIS TRAINING.' David was too frail to run alongside and wave. There's no movie scene to imagine here, as I guess he just turned and walked away, as abruptly as a branch cut from a tree, falling. Where did he and Tina go to afterwards, I wonder, as I stand and watch modern commuters rushing to make their voluntary trains. Buy a coffee, maybe, or something stronger. If I had to leave my son Ezra at a station, sending him off into the utter unknown, I would buy two bottles of red wine, some whisky and a packet of cigarettes, check into the Motel One high up on the corrugated iron arm, or whatever seedy equivalent I could find, and sit on a still-made bed until I fell asleep on thin carpeted hotel floor, only waking to check out late morning, and try, somehow, to return to my life.

I assume I will never have to do that.

When my great-grandfather David Schapira came to Vienna in the autumn of 1914, from a part of East Galicia which was then Polish, part of the Austro-Hungarian Empire, and is now in Ukraine, he was fascinated by the place. Totally awed by the city he had settled in – as an impressionable country boy, startled alive by teeming crowds and busy traffic, like the bit where Alice meets Wonderland. So much rush and noise and colour that, despite being overwhelmed and rather afraid, you can't imagine ever wanting to go back. He writes in his memoir of long tours he took of the 'great ring road and through the inner city', plus trips to Kahlenberg mountain for views of his new world; plus the

Prater, where the big red ferris wheel they use in *The Third Man* spins tourists around and around, proudly looming above rickety fairground rides that would have been wooden in David's time, but are largely neon now. The main stench there, I recall, was sausage and vomit. My great-grandfather walked along meadows by the banks of the river Danube, near where I would later go to school, all the way up to Grinzing, a cobbled coach-party trap where the snap-happy can take photos of a bland white building Beethoven once called home.

David was in Vienna because of the Russians. He was born on 29 December 1897 in a small village called Stojanow, sixty miles away from the larger town of Rava-Ruska. He moved to the latter in his early teens. Much in the region where he spent his youth was then steeped in Jewish tradition and building. He writes that his family – my ancestors – were from a 'hardy stock of deeply religious eastern European Jews', something which, as often is the case, can lead to persecution and flight.

When the heir to the Austro-Hungarian Empire was shot in Sarajevo, many settled lives stopped being so. The continent-wide disruption put an end to my great-grandfather's enjoyment of the long summer he had been looking forward to after big exams. He was sixteen at the time and, as he dictated years later, of the events that led to over four years of brutal, rotten conflict and 10 million refugees: 'The occurrences which followed in quick succession [after Ferdinand's death] concerning ultimatums and Russian threats of war and military preparation stimulated growing uneasiness and fear near the Russian border.'

The threats increased and soldiers stationed in Rava-Ruska took up positions in full battle gear before war was even declared. Everyone knew what was coming.

'Patrols of Cossacks were sighted in forested hills north of the town . . .' reads the memoir. 'An increasing numbers of passenger and freight trains passed through the normally busy terminal of Rava-Ruska, carrying military personnel, armaments and refugees.'

The Schapira family fled. They feared the Russians and the inevitable pogrom – which is another word for massacre and is usually anti-Semitic. Many were forced to stay, though, and face the uncertainty, as money was needed to leave, while some who did get out would later return, only to die by the guns of the Nazis in the next war; shot, tumbling into mass graves. My ancestors in 1914 stuck to back routes rather than a main road; at least a day of travelling.

'It was a very depressing sight. We found hundreds of people from our town, frightened off by threat of Russian invasion, passing along the narrow country lane with wheelbarrows loaded with a few of their most important possessions and with which they were trying to reach the next safe haven before nightfall.'

He emphasises urgency, but his prose never rises above an unspectacular tone that's so powerful when describing the spectacular. 'The next day,' he says of an early part of the flight, almost as a mutter, 'we saw the first casualties.'

Word spread that a battle taking place in a small town outside of Lviv was going well for the local population. It was an offshoot of the Battle of Lviv, which started about the time of David's escape with his family. A struggle between Russians and Austro-Hungarians, it was waged for three weeks from 23 August 1914, resulting in the loss of 650,000 soldiers' lives. The battle didn't end well for David's side, though, with Russia victorious and subsequently ruling eastern Galicia for most of the next year.

'In this way,' he writes, referring to his imminent conscription into the Austro-Hungarian army, just months after settling in Vienna, 'I experienced as a refugee the changing front lines of the war which I was later to experience at first hand as a soldier at the front one and a half years later.'

They made it out of Galicia on a military freight train, with spots secured by a bribe, on a carriage with a sign reading '40 men or 6 horses'. The first of two times – with only a twenty-five-year gap in between – that an ancestor of mine made it out alive by train, from a home that didn't want them. There is appreciation and humour from both of them on the way to safety being achieved. Heinz was rude about the Dutch landscape, of course; while his father describes his own refugee journey like they are on a well-planned road-trip of up-market east European spa resorts. There is, apparently, a 'very nice small town' on the outskirts of the Carpathian mountains that he passed through and, among the doom, there is a real sense of adventure; like the girl I saw on the news who was fleeing Syria in a wheelchair and treating her journey like a magical tour. She had, she beamed, never even been in a boat before.

Parallels to today are always a google-flit away. On 3 October 1914, David and his family of ten arrived in Vienna, after weeks of waiting, travelling, and waiting some more. 'The sight of turbulent and jostling crowds of people filling the eastern railway terminal was over-whelming.' One hundred and one years later, on a news website: 'VIENNA Train stations with thousands fleeing war in Asia, the middle-east have characterised Europe's refugee crisis . . . At the Austrian capital's main train station, an initially small volunteer effort to provide humanitarian aid has grown – and turned the station into a refugee hub. Volunteers started with a couple of tables of snacks, but now serve up to 3,000 people three meals a day.'

In 2016, largely in reaction to news stories like that, Austria very, very nearly elected Norbert Hofer to be their President. The leader of the Freedom Party, who you would put in a sentence with Marine Le Pen and Nigel Farage, said of their recent influx of asylum seekers, 'we are not the world's social department.' In addition, he says, under photos of him grinning with his right arm well raised, generalising contentedly about an entire section of asylum seekers, that: 'To those in Austria who go to war for Islamic State, or rape women, I say to those people: "This is not your home."' And so a new generation of Austrians have a racist lie thrust upon them about a group of wholly different people, planting seeds for either flowers or weeds, depending on how much they listen to Hofer and who they then talk to and read. Back in 1914, according to my great-grandfather, Vienna was already densely populated and many who lived there didn't think there was room for him and his family, and the ever-increasing numbers of their desperate kind.

'The non-Jewish population was definitely not favourably disposed towards the Jewish war refugees,' he explains, and only the generosity of a random local led to David's father finding two rooms to take them in. That family of ten, by the way, included a 'baby born en-route', barely mentioned with more than a passing nod. When all life is drama, I suppose, a birth on a refugee trail, to a large family in desperate need of safety, just isn't that big a deal.

His memories are of other things. As a teenager, he probably wasn't that interested in his umpteenth sibling. And with no schools for Polish speakers in Vienna, David spent early days just walking about. That ring road, palace-next-to-palace where even the town hall looks like a fairytale castle; those are the sights that stayed with him, that made it into his memoir decades later. A blossoming time when all he saw was taken in and remembered. He seems happy, interested, as his son would be in London a couple of decades later when the next flight of my family had to happen. Both men, it seems, are optimists dealt a bad hand, filled with relief. Or fortitude. Or luck. A whole host of words too varied to list here.

'I not only became familiar with Vienna,' reads the memoir, 'but also learned to love it, and adopted it as my second home.'

Why did I pick Vienna to use as a metaphor for the rest of your life? My father lives in Vienna now. I had to track him down. I didn't see him from the time I was eight til I was about 23–24 years old. He lives in Vienna, Austria, which I thought was rather bizarre because he left Germany in the first place because of this guy named Hitler and he ends up going to the same place Hitler hung out all those years! Vienna, for a long time was the crossroads. During the Cold War between the Eastern Bloc, the Warsaw Pact nations and the NATO countries was the city of Vienna . . . Vienna was always the crossroads, between the Ottoman Empire and the Holy Roman Empire. So the metaphor of Vienna has the meaning of a crossroad. A place of exchange – it's the place where cultures co-mingle. You get great beer in Vienna, but you also get brandy from Armenia. It was a place where cultures co-mingled.

So said Billy Joel once, on his live album *An Evening of Questions and Answers . . . and Perhaps a Few Songs*, of his song 'Vienna'. A long quote that makes perfect historical sense until you reach that optimistic last sentence, which – over the past century onwards – from David's arrival as a Jew to the arrival of refugees from the Middle East, seems to be anything but true. If there is co-mingling, it is obscured – leaving instead a place, like most European cities, where cultures arrive and face antagonism and distrust from people who already live there. David arrived in 1914 and, by 1933, his dream of living an unthreatened life in his adopted second home was over.

He married Tina in the summer of 1920, after meeting her a year earlier, and the couple and their two boys, Heinz and Rudi, lived the normal city life. David was a lawyer and had income from a small tobacconist's shop too, plus a pension given to blind veterans from the First World War. But the country had started descending into what would, on 7 August 1939, make him and his wife lead their sons to Westbahnhof.

David's memoir covers the historical basics. In the summer of 1933 there were violent clashes between fascists and social democrats, 'bloody battles in Vienna with a character of a civil war', he explains, a little wearily. ('I have been here before!') It only became worse. Attempted putsches and actual clashes, plus the 'radicalisation of internal political life . . . and an increasing economic crisis which was brought about by bank crashes, accompanied by mass-unemployment'. The disenfranchised needed a scapegoat, and as fascism rose on major borders with Italy and Germany, pressure was exerted on a government so weak that Hitler was able to march an army in to 'almost a jubilant reception' on 11 March 1938 – the exact point their home began to feel more like a house they needed to move out of.

Less than a month later, everything that could stigmatise and threaten Jews was put into action thanks to a mix of the Race Laws and general madness. Public humiliation and detention; 'untold numbers sent to German concentration camps at Dachau and Buchenwald, where many suffered and died miserably'; his sons were made to leave their state school; 'I was not allowed to enter my tobacconist shop or give any instructions concerning the running of the business to the shop assistant I employed, or to take any of the monthly profits. My tobacconist's licence was taken away.' He was struck off the list of lawyers too and couldn't represent Aryan clients. He writes of Kristallnacht: 'Synagogues and Jewish shops were set in flames, Jews were dragged out of their homes, brutally beaten, murdered, arrested without cause and deported.'

Pogroms started in early 1941, twenty-seven years after the pogroms he had left home in Rava-Ruska to avoid. His sons had gone by then, and were testing out their new lives in England while the Jews they had left behind in Vienna were forced to wear the Star of David, with a thousand a week being deported to Poland.

'In the first days,' recalls David, whose own fate would come a little later, of the humiliation of pinning a star to his coat, 'it was like running a gauntlet to go out in the street. Even Aryan friends would not dare to greet Jewish acquaintances, let alone speak to them or have any other personal contact with them.'

So much for his second home and the city he loved.

Two blocks before the Schapira family home that has long since been cleared of my ancestors, a streetlight has a clear plastic bag tied around it holding copies of national newspaper *Österreich*. 'Österreich Loves Österreich!' boasts a red-and-white slogan and, off to the left, on the Sunday morning I visit, pushing Ezra in his buggy while my wife Rosamund used maps on her phone to find a way, I spot graffiti of a swastika and a big caps scrawl of the word Nazi, arm-span high.

'Depressing,' I say, taking a photo.

Rosamund takes our son off me and walks on, shaking her head and sighing. I follow and spot more graffiti, this time of a smiling penis but in the same style and curvature as the swastika. It's the same artist's self-portrait, I assume.

Fast cars make use of empty Sunday streets, on this quiet and narrow road – with tall buildings that block out crisp sun and cast cold shadows on the ground. A lady hangs out of a first-floor window and stares. Some blocks have been tarted up, one with smart glass balconies at the bottom of the hill, which runs towards the ring road, edging away from the poorer end where kebab shops and main roads fight for space with tram-lines and cheap clothes shops. But it is mostly brown or grey all over, the only bright colour coming from a Penny Markt. It isn't an interesting, even particularly describable road. This is all I've got.

Number 14 is no different. There are thirty-one flats in its six-floor building, and I am not sure what number my family lived in. Nobody is. The front door to the whole lot is smart and black metal, surrounded by a decoration of embossed flowers, in front of a window to marble stairs that are so worn they don't seem to have been replaced since Heinz and David's day. Same goes for the round handle, tired to a metal shine, so I place my fingers on its surface and touch it as they would have. It's meant to be a magical moment, sparks of inspiration and a connection to the past, but I just worry that someone who lives there now will need to get in, so I move on, awkwardly looking back at the woman across the street, now smoking and staring. Really, there's nothing there. It's simply a building and, as with all homes, its history sits inside, through the doors humans enter and leave in order to make memories kept in by their four walls. Some eventful, some dull, but all, hopefully, private unless you don't want them to be. And everybody, really, wants secrets to remain so.

In a photo album kept by Heinz until his death, and passed down to my mum and her sister, my aunt Fiona, all the pictures from 1938–39 are blissful and happy. There is a class of students sitting in the sun, reading, smiling. There are eleven of them, up against a wall. Some posing, some grinning. The usual teenage image. In summer, they would take lessons outside and one photo of a geography class looks like a painting. Shirt sleeves rolled up, lying around in a courtyard. A louche place to learn. The next photo shows a boy called Georg smoking a cigarette while another is of a Schnapps party, where Heinz and friends sit and play cards. In spring 1939, there is a trip to Hohe Mandling in the hills outside the city. The countdown clock gets louder, to their departure. On 30 July, a photo captioned 'Letzter Sonntag im Wienerwald' (last Sunday in Wienerwald). He knew what was happening by now. All his documents were in order. The next photo shows my grandfather in Hyde Park.

The day of parting, desired and yet not desired, has arrived' [he wrote in his diary when he left Vienna for London]. With a laughing face and heavy, oh so heavy heart I say farewell to the apartment where I was born – the place of my childhood and early youth. Will I ever see it again? Don't think! Shall I describe our parting? I shall never forget it; it was too terrible. Such misery! Just curse! Curse! We all wept terribly; the worst was father crying! Only Rudi seemed cheerful, but when the train left the station I found him leaning out of the other window crying bitterly. Who can bear it!?

By Cologne, teenage excitement had kicked in, their parents a sad thought that would hit them from time to time.

When I left home for university, my parents stayed a night at a hotel near my campus. Not to check up on me, thankfully – that would have been embarrassing, seeing as I had given up on making new friends way before midnight and was sat up in bed listening to sad songs, sipping a cup of tea, missing home. Rather, they stayed away from our house in Surrey as my sister had left three years before and my mum didn't want to go back to a nest both her birds had flown. Of course, the next day, she had to. They couldn't live in a converted stately home in Warwickshire for ever. She opened the door to my bedroom, with its band posters on the wall and Airfix aeroplanes still on the ceiling, and burst into tears.

After Heinz and Rudi fled Vienna, the only

communication between them and their parents was via letter sent through an aunt in neutral Holland. Then Holland was invaded in May 1940 and communication was only possible in brief and impersonal Red Cross telegrams. It's striking how much that home in Hohl-weggasse is brought up by the parents. The importance of a physical place full of memories that helps to ground emotions running amok. I only have letters from Vienna to London, found in my aunt's loft. The ones Heinz and Rudi sent were lost in boxes decades ago, in a packed-up flat, but all the secrets and tics that made their family, like any family, who they are, are there. Nicknames. Nagging. Conversations meant for their own four walls, spilt into the open. Many, of course, being read by officials intercepting the mail. Nothing belonged to them any more.

One day after they left for England, on 8 August 1939, Tina wrote a letter to her two sons. 'My dear beloved boys!' it begins. She tells them that she needs the comfort of their words and hopes they will have written to her on the way to London.

It is so lonely and desolate without you. The flat is strange and cold . . . Every object and word reminds us of you and brings such big heartache . . . After your poor, good Papa returned from the train, he fell on your bed, my dear Heinzerl . . . He kissed the mattress and cried, 'My child lay here!' I don't dare to put your things in order. That would still hurt too much. I promise you, however, that everything that was dear and familiar to you will have a place of honour in our house and be cared for faithfully by me until I am able to hand them over to you again . . . I am convinced, however, it will only take a few days for you to be enthusiastic about the new and wonderful things you are going to experience . . . Sleep well, my dear children, thousand kisses to you both.

A second letter is undated, but thanks Heinz for a ten-page letter he sent. David, they write, had been with a client when it arrived, but he made excuses immediately and husband and wife read it together. The letter from England must have brought them good news, as the parents seem happy: 'I think it is absolutely necessary you both have your suits pressed, even if you have to save on something else . . . A well-dressed person will surely be more successful than someone who is sloppily dressed.' Then David and Tina are angry at Rudi for no more than 'a couple of thoughtless greetings' compared to his swot younger brother's mass of detail and information and care. They explain that they are keeping themselves busy. 'Work is the best medicine for a broken heart.' ('PS – How are you managing without underwear?') In another, their grandmother writes: 'Since you both have been away, it is very, very sad here. I no longer have anybody whom I scold nor anyone whom I can forgive. I envy you, my two bad boys, that you are far away.' A month and a bit later, David and Tina write to say that a close relative has gone missing, and that their grandmother spends most days in tears. Letter number 23 is sent on 28 November 1939. That's twenty-three in less than four months, but a lot aren't getting through, gone astray, and so the parents promise to do more, write more, better the odds, distract themselves from empty rooms.

> In answer to the question about our lovely flat, [writes Tina] I can say nothing has changed in it and it is, as always, the loveliest little spot on earth, because we lived the best and happiest days of our lives in it, because it was your home in your childhood and youth, and because it is the place about which you think when parents, country and home are mentioned. Everything is still in its old place: school books are in the desk as if you were still going to school – all your library is meticulously ordered and stamps are lovingly kept and stored; as are your small everyday things such as notebooks, pencils, pens, set-squares. Perhaps someday we will be able to bring you all these things, if we should be lucky enough to visit. For the present, however, we feel happiest amongst our own four walls and even though we are also very lonely within them, each spot is blessed nevertheless with the memory of your presence.

In the margins another relative, who calls Heinz and Rudi nephews, makes a first mention of camps. People they knew had been sent to the camps and were being 'well looked after', even though they couldn't write. A letter from before Christmas, from David, isn't stamped in Britain until the middle of January.

Just remain so assured, clever, and brave, then all unpleasantness of these ugly times, will be an episode out of which you save the positive elements for the future and consider negative aspects no more than a bad dream ... The most important thing is we survive this war and – with God's help – and through my active support you will be able to continue on and broaden a path in your lives which your talents and wishes have marked out for you.

David and Tina left presents out on the kitchen table for the boys, which, they write, they will save to pass onto them later, whenever that may be.

Forty minutes outside Vienna is the tranquil and tiny town of Fischauer, with an outdoor natural swimming pool complex called the Thermalbad. I thought Thermal meant heated when I drove Rosamund and Ezra there on a chilly spring day, saying how lucky we were that the water was warm, because imagine swimming outdoors in this weather.

When we arrived, the pools were empty. Pretty, but empty. Translucent and calming, but empty. There were rows and rows of yellow-and-green changing huts and a couple of cafés, one open, but no people other than an attendant at the till who was surprised to see anybody. Barely bothering to crawl out of her boredom, she gave us a couple of tickets and we went into the grounds. It looked enticing. Fresh cut lawn flowed into a distant line of trees and the quiet enveloped us. Just birdsong and, after one dip in the water, the realisation that Thermal doesn't mean heated.

There is a photo of my grandfather in Fischauer Thermalbad from 1933, in front of the very same changing huts that still stand, on a diving board that is no longer there. That year, of course, was when Vienna began to feel as threatening to David as his old home in Rava-Ruska had, back in 1914. But until then, Austria had been a playground for his son, allowed freedom of movement because his father had fled years before. Six years after that photo by the outdoor pool was taken, Heinz and his brother had to flee too.

News comes, fairly constantly these days, of a rise of anti-Semitism in Britain. The first few months of 2015 were headline ones for Jews. Bad headlines; the kind that spin up as a montage on a cinema screen, to short-hand that things aren't going well. One day, the front of *The Times* had as its main image a sombre photo of British Jews in a synagogue. 'Community in fear: British Jews show solidarity after the Paris attacks. The home secretary warned yesterday of a surge of anti-Semitism in Britain.' That was the week after the terrorist assault on a Jewish deli in Paris, days after the *Charlie Hebdo* cartoonists were shot. A random look at Twitter one day revealed a poster on a London bus stop for an event marking Holocaust Memorial Day, defaced with the graffiti, 'LIARS'. A short video on the *Guardian* website was about a Polish far right party called the National Radical Camp. 'Polish land only in Polish hands!' they chanted. They are Nazis, and men and women with balaclavas throw rocks at other men and women in a street full of broken glass and steam. Common scenes. They shout 'War!' There are articles I read arguing anti-Semitism in Britain isn't as bad as scare stories suggest. That it is most dangerous in France. There is a joke about how the toughest thing to happen to Jews in Britain is some golf clubs are exclusionary. I don't know if that's true. I'm not Jewish.

However, that said, I do come from a 'hardy stock of deeply religious eastern European Jews', three generations back. Perhaps, for some people, my blood has not been diluted enough; perhaps I have no place on this Aryan island either. There are people on the right all over the world who think like this. On the day Donald Trump won the American presidential election, his supporter Ann Coulter tweeted, 'If only people with at least four grandparents born in America were voting, Trump would win in a 50-state landslide.' Regardless of whether that is true, one of my grandparents was born in a country different to mine. There are people who think that makes me too foreign.

One search in that cesspool of Twitter, a digital realm for journalists and the lonely, brings up opinions like, 'Do you expect Jews to be constantly coddled, pandered to? Jews ought to be treated with the disdain they deserve'; 'Jews have been a menace to mankind . . . A plague on culture and civilisation'; 'Jews control Britain and are committing genocide on us'. Then there are the facts: a 25 per cent rise in anti-Semitic offences in 2015; a mob shouting 'Kill the Jews' outside a synagogue in north London, smashing up property and attacking worshippers. Many of these slogans and actions appear to come from young people. We live in times of economic uncertainty where scapegoats are looked for and found. Let's blame someone different from us. Anti-Semitism is of personal interest because, if my grandfather were still alive, which is entirely possible had he not had cancer in the mid-1980s, then trolls and worse would be talking about him, threatening him. And he was white. The attitude towards the new wave of Muslim refugees is worse. They often have a different skin colour. They often dress differently. They most certainly are not British, some think, as narrow as that definition could be. That is why so many want to stop them from coming in, regardless of the wars that are being waged back in their homelands.

There is, after all, no more room.

That's how David felt the Viennese felt about him, when he got to Vienna in 1914. Over the next nineteen years, though, he became one of them. Some may have snivelled behind his back and not wanted him to be there, but in better times, those voices are muted. Only economic issues and the arrival of Hitler meant his being a Jew became a problem again, so much so that he had to move his sons thousands of miles away to a place they had never been, on a train through the country where what he was making them run from had begun. How extraordinary to experience such a decline in circumstance. When I read his memoir, on occasion, in the happier bits, it reads like something that I could have written over the past decade, but then forgot about.

'My marriage and family life were harmonious and

happy,' he says of the era that began in the 1920s and nudged its way into the 30s.

> My sons, who were well-adjusted, intelligent, hand-some and amiable, were good pupils and loving children. Through her bright personality, gentle intelligence and hospitality, my wife ensured a pleasant social life at home with a small group of cheerful and gregarious friends, especially musically interested people of the same age . . . who contributed greatly to pleasant and stimulating evenings. Evenings, school holidays and holidays were all arranged in a pleasant and useful manner, with a view to the development and the interests of the children. This peaceful, happy and well-ordered family life, however, was disturbed by the changes at the beginning of the 1930s.

That pretty much describes my life. A busy, fun mix of family, work and having friends over for dinner where I will bore them about Radiohead. And I wonder if I, or any of my friends, or Ezra, who we named in honour of the sacrifices his family made, will ever face great change or abuse in their lives.

Chapter 3

When Yousef Abdul, 16, arrived in Austria from Iraq, his school teacher asked him to write up a project about his experiences. He emailed it to me the day after we met in his tiny studio home in the south-west of Vienna, on a May day so hot people walked barefoot on chipped pavements to keep the sweat from their shoes.

'After a long suffering of war and explosions,' he wrote, 'and especially threats suffered by my mother we decided to travel to a safe country . . . We were so afraid and could not see anything. There was another boat behind us, but it sank . . . Then God saved us . . . At last, we have arrived here.'

That's the basics of what he wrote and for the first time in a long time, he told me, he, his mother and younger sister all felt secure. But, yes, the above extract is the essence of what is in his project, and it's strange that people need more.

My grandfather Heinz went to the Franz Jozef Real-gymnasium, in the middle of Vienna. It is a school that still exists in the same grand building, down a quiet pedestrianised side street where smoking students take a break from exams to huddle by cycle racks out the front, gossiping and puffing under a pair of two-storey-high flags. One the red and white of the Austrian flag, the other the blue and yellow of the European Union. The closest station to the school was closed the day I visited, so, instead, I walked from the city's smartest stop in the old park of Stadtpark, a forest-green space that curls around a top corner of the central ring road like an eighties shoulder pad. I used to travel past it every day on the way to school, up the U4 to Schwedenplatz, to change to the U1, and take that all the way to the end, past the UN headquarters on the river Danube. The International School I went to was up in the north-east of the city. It is where I spent some formative years of my early teens; first kiss, only fight, weeks-on-weeks of talking back to all the teachers, and once tripped over a kerb and broke my finger.

Stadtpark, like much of Vienna's architecture, hasn't changed in centuries. It is a city much like Miss Havisham, sitting all trussed up expecting effort to be made for her, by others, not really fussed about whether people come to visit or not. Recently, some of this has changed with a relatively hip museums quarter, plus an area of warehouses that acts like Berlin's kid brother. But, mostly, as will always be the case with a small city most famous for opera and classical music, and which did not have to be rebuilt after the war, it feels old and regal. A bit stuffy and certainly not cool. A municipal equivalent of Martin Scorsese's period drama *The Age of Innocence*, and proud of that status too.

Yet its absence of visible reinvention has a tacit

benefit. By looking very old – a blend of Romanesque, Baroque and Art Nouveau – it skips the last century of history for locals and tourists alike. Look, here is a hotel that has sold one of the most famous chocolate cakes in the world since 1876. The gleaming bronze statue on the main route through Stadtpark is of Johann Strauß, who died in 1899. If you want to take a tour of the ring road, you can do so either by tram or horse and carriage. Either way, you are not doing anything you could not have done decades before the television was invented. A lot of history was made in Vienna between 1914 and 1939 and, while the music made in that era is still played to coach loads of tourists, most of the politics is swept under the surface. It is entirely feasible to visit the city and not realise its people were affected by either of the world wars. Just have a nice walk instead, eat strudel while tipping waiters dressed in lederhosen and dirndl.

Walking through the park from Stadtpark station to the school, I retrace steps my grandfather would have taken each day. It's such a fine walk. Well-cut pathways and manicured trees. Stalls flogging fizz and posh jams. Flowerbeds full of plants very specifically planned to be there. My grandfather walked this way for years, and he worked hard, too. His grades were good. In the school, I meet a teacher and the head, who show off a report card from 1938, kept for decades in archives. His name and address and other details of his life are there scrawled in ink, and it's weird to see. Moving too, of course. A little humbling. German; Latin; French; Maths; Religion; History; Geography; Natural History;

Chemistry. All '*gut*', some '*sehr gut*', with English, usefully, particularly highly marked. We flick to the front of the book to see what he and the rest of his class from that year managed in their spring exams. He did very well again, but whereas most of the others, bar a couple, took four exams, he had scores for only three.

'Why?' I ask, making a joke about him sleeping in.

Solemnly, we turn back to his individual page, and a margin on the right where it says, on 28 April 1939, that Heinz left school. He and the other Jews, who also didn't sit that fourth exam, were told to stand and leave in the middle of class. The final test was after they had gone. For the last year he was in Vienna, my grandfather went to Zwi-Perez-Chajes Schule, a Jewish school significantly further away from his flat and a brutal example of how, just as you don't move house to save a relationship, you can't move to a different school in the same city during a fascist rule and hope that you will be free.

I read the foreword to the school's annual report from 1938.

First, all Jewish teachers were dismissed, putting to an end the shameful and unnatural arrangement whereby Jews teach Aryan children . . . shortly afterwards the separation of Aryan and Jewish children was completed. For the first time since its foundation, our establishment was free of Jews and the change could be felt – pure, fresh air streamed in. On April 29th, we could receive the District II Aryan pupils who had been allocated to us; the school was now ready to fulfil any major task the National Socialist state required.

The Franz Jozef Realgymnasium doesn't hide this. I notice reminders as I leave, of how, to its great credit, unlike the city it sits in and serves, the administration takes to shouting about its history in an effort to try and make sure it doesn't happen again. Their students are a metropolitan mash-up of immigration and faith. It is better than doing nothing, I suppose, even if children have been taught about past atrocities for ever to such little avail. I shove open the heavy front door to the sunlight outside, and turn to read the stencils that cover it, flowing off the end of one line onto the next, spelling slogans for anyone walking by or in.

The one at the top is by Friedrich Hacker, who Wikipedia tells me, via Google Translate, is a 'US/American/Austrian psychiatrist, psychoanalyst and researcher of aggression'. His short quote is cute – 'Violence is simple. Alternatives to violence are complex' – and reads like a punk slogan. It is an international T-shirt brand's pinching away from ubiquity. The quote below, however, is unwieldy. Written by the Austrian writer Karl Kraus – Jonathan Franzen is a fanboy – it is significantly harder to translate, with the closest gist I have being that words are often interpreted in different ways and that 'a word holds several thoughts'.

I don't think that's true.

That report and order from 1938 can't be interpreted in any other way and, as I walk back through Stadtpark, past teenagers of many races playing ball games in the heat, as settled in their education as my grandfather was on 27 April 1938, this idea of Kraus, that words can be interpreted differently, feels like an excuse. Words are not hard. They are easy to understand once they are spoken. That's the point of words and it is, instead, silence that allows several thoughts to fester.

Vienna is full of silence, its troubled history making as much noise as the spare room in your house. Take Berlin for instance. It has a Holocaust memorial so vast is takes up an entire square, halfway between two of the city's major tourist attractions. You cannot avoid it. Vienna, however, is just old statues of composers and posh cake in marble cafés. That is what people go to the city for and the city doesn't want them, or their own people, to be reminded of a pitiful past that kicked its own citizens out of school. No wonder half the population voted for the far right in 2016. They have probably forgotten that anything bad happened last time.

In a café where the average age of the clientele is 103, I meet Adham Alrumhain for black coffee and cigarettes. I don't even smoke, but when a man in the middle of a story about a 2,000-mile, death-nearing journey by land, foot and dinghy from Syria to Austria holds out one of his Marlboro Lights, it is rude to turn it down. Sparked up and sitting at a cramped circular table in a garden by the road, our knees touch as we make small talk about transport, weather, the 'two-storey bus' when I tell him that I live in London. Needless to say, his is the only non-white face around. The café is in the district of

CHAPTER 3

Hietzing, next to Schönbrunn palace; a place so touristy it's basically Habsburg Disneyland. Most people sport wizard-white hair, half of them hold open maps and nearly everyone is tucking into those famous strudels; the scratchy sound of metal fork on china plate the one noise in a café stuffed with visitors and local couples, who seem to have long since run out of things to talk about.

Adham is a tall, stocky man in a tight, dark T-shirt with a NAVY slogan, carrying a plastic folder and an iPhone, white headphones dangling over shoulders. A normal twenty-five-year-old, then, but he is more jittery than most men of his age I have known – at least the ones who weren't coming down. Looking over his shoulder and over my shoulder. Not twitchy as such – there is more purpose to his gaze as he scopes out the shadows.

He had been in Vienna for eighteen months when we met. An accidental country for a young refugee who left Damascus hoping to reach Holland. Fifteen days in Turkey, two-and-a-half months in Greece. Twenty days on the road from Greece to Austria. He had a friend in The Netherlands and his friend had six brothers there. They would have sorted each other out with work and homes. But he was caught by police in Vienna and couldn't go any further. I ask what he knew of Austria before he settled here, and he shakes his head. Nothing at all. 'Alps, snow, Vienna. Lakes and stuff . . .' he says with a shrug. 'Actually, I wanted sea. I love sea. But I was caught.' At the top end of a landlocked country, he couldn't be further from the sea. But he knows he is one of the lucky ones. He was picked up by authorities when he and fellow refugees were taking a break from their smuggler's car somewhere in the capital – where exactly he cannot quite remember, because he was so tired. He corrects himself. He cannot remember where it was at all. Zombies across a pitch-black continent they had only seen on films. The refugees walked across a road and two federal officers stopped them.

'We were five people,' says Adham, sadly. 'We were dirty and muddy and stuff, so they came and asked for passports. We didn't have any. They said this is your last destination. I was really depressed for two days.'

The five were kept in jail, but when a translator came to help, they were moved to Styria; a beautiful and mountainous province south of Vienna. From sound alone, you might think it was picked for the Syrians to feel, almost, at home. Shifting someone from Norwich to Northwich, if you like. When he finishes his university course in the capital, where he is training to be an English and German translator, he would like to return there. The countryside is like The Shire. The air is clear. But the problem, I think, is it's even less cosmopolitan than Vienna. A place with small towns where, I imagine, given time, he would find it too difficult being different.

I ask how well he's settling in, mixing with Austrians, making a home. 'Trying to,' he says. There is an organisation that welcomes new immigrants and sets up events to assimilate them into a society that seems split halfway between the far-right and decency.

'There are parties,' he says. 'Where there are the lovers and the haters . . .' He stops, before correcting himself.

'Not lovers, actually. Rather they accept us. But I get a lot of confrontations from haters . . . They shout . . . But, it was very expensive to come here, when we came . . . I didn't have any choice. I wish that I was now in Syria, but I can't be.'

The reasons are simple. Adham was living in Damascus and studying, delaying the legal requirement to join the army. He was allowed to delay that order if he was in higher education, so he stayed in higher education and kept putting back the time that he would be forced to join until the day a friend's father, a man with high-up military connections, told him he couldn't delay any more. Everyone must fight. He was advised to run away, as he had only forty days remaining on his passport and that wouldn't be renewed. He took a flight as soon as he could. He left because he didn't want to join the army, but it's deeper than that. It's not all white flowers and conscientious objection. If he had stayed and been conscripted, he says, he would have been sent to fight Isis, and he is a Christian.

'So, they put us on the firing line,' he says, emotionlessly.

The Sunnis and the Christians, he repeats, they are put at the front of the Syrian army as cannon fodder. And he is tall and big. Strapping, in fact. You could call him a tree trunk to his face if you were brave enough. So, his friend's military father told him there was no way he wouldn't be right at the front of his unit on day one of his service and no way that he wouldn't be shot. He didn't want to leave, but his mother told him to. She left as well, for reasons to do with staying alive, and she went to Germany for four months. When I met Adham, she was back in Syria.

'What's it like?'

'It's hell.'

'Are you optimistic?'

'*Nein* . . . I said *nein*!'

He's trying to fit in. He lights a cigarette. His mother is afraid all the time. She went home because she didn't have friends in Germany and wanted to be somewhere where she knows where everything is.

'She feels alone now.'

Adham paid €10,000 to travel from Turkey to Holland – with no refund offered if he didn't make it that far. He owned four flats. Like my great-grandfather David and grandfather Heinz, he was a decently-off man from a decently-off family with the means to escape. He sold one of his flats and a car, the money given to smugglers and spent on his transport. He tells me there were ninety-one people in the small boat that took him to Greece. Then he walked from Greece to Macedonia, before taking a train to the border with Serbia and walking five hours to another smuggler's house. From there, it was a twenty-hour hike up to the borders, but on four occasions police caught them and sent them back. On and on. On and on. He said he barely ate for five days. But he was lucky. The smugglers, he says, come from many different countries and religions, many belonging to gangs on the make from misery. Many refugees have phones and money stolen. They're beaten. At least their blood reaches European soil. But Adham's group was big, and therefore they made it.

Adham is big, too. That, and his religion, are the main reasons he had to leave Syria in the first place, lest he be shot.

And yet he doesn't feel welcome here. That's clear from how nervous he is. 'It depends on the people. There is a lot of generalising. Rape incidents and stealing, killing . . . They say that is from all refugees . . . They see us and think we are the same person. Ten days ago, I was with my Austrian friend in a disco and we went for a smoke . . . One guy stood in front of me and pushed me and I cannot really fight back unless he hits me. So I kept calm and said, "What's wrong?" Then he pushed me again. Then his friends came and they were going to hit me, so I had to hit back.'

He is scared to tell me this but he can't stop. That sort of violent and unprovoked attack happened three times in the few weeks he was living in Styria. He says he always tries to reason with his aggressors, but they simply don't care. How old are they? 'From seventeen to sixty,' he says, so he might as well have said 'everybody'. He can take and nearly accept the middle fingers sticking up from car windows, but the violence, not so much.

'Why?' he says, in high-pitched panic. 'I didn't do anything.'

'Do you feel safer here?'

'Hmm. I should define safe. If you mean peace of mind, I had more in Syria.'

'Really?'

'Yes. I was living a nice life.'

Perhaps the most telling moment of our meeting

came at the end. The coffees cost €6. Not so much, but I gestured, rightly, to pay. He had travelled through Vienna to meet me at my convenience and sat, for an hour, telling me about his very difficult life. He had given me a cigarette. I held out a €10 note to the old white waiter. Adham pushed my hand away. I pushed it forward. He pushed it away. We frowned at each other a couple of times. We moved into hard frowns. He insisted. I insisted, and this went on for long enough to test the waiter's patience. Adham would not back down. I, for a while, would not back down either, but I realised this wasn't going to end with me paying the bill. It simply meant more to him. He wanted to impress the waiter, who could not have looked more stereotypically Austrian. He wasn't doing it to impress me, but, rather, the country he had found himself in. If he pays, he is making an effort and a contribution. He is being normal. A three-part mix of effort, shame and fear fuelled that desire to pay, and he left a tip too. I suppose his thinking went, *If Austrians see me buying things in their country then, maybe, they will think I can be like them and they will stop hitting me in the face and let me belong here.*

Finally, I ask him how many of the people he met on his long journey from Syria to Austria wanted to travel across the whole of Europe and end up in England. He thinks about it, adding up memories and encounters. I wonder if the figure he is totting up will prove the anti-immigration faction right about the swarm, the influx, the overstuffing of our island.

'How many wanted to come to England?' he asks.

66

'Yes.'

'One.'

On his first morning in his new country, in a room at 10 Windermere Avenue in north-west London, my grandfather Heinz woke at ten. He was knackered. Forty hours without sleep going near non-stop across Europe at a pelt would do that to anybody. He, though, could finally feel rested, even a little at ease, able to sleep in without fearing that the door would be kicked down.

'That's very kind of London,' he scrawled in his diary on 9 August 1939 and he means he is grateful for a lie-in, but added weight is easily and posthumously applied. The paragraphs tag-team English and German – more of the latter earlier on, far more of the former as he settles and learns more. On that first day, he and his older brother Rudi – who was staying in the same house – had to head south to Bloomsbury House, to meet fellow refugee Mary at half-past two. It was an administrative centre that had been set up for incoming Jews. Breakfast before they left was 'tea, milk, bread and butter, eggs and something like honey,' Heinz writes, and, after two hours of queuing in front of a desk, they left the registration building to enjoy London's postcard sights: St James's Palace, Buckingham Palace, County Hall, Parliament, Westminster, before going back to Windermere Avenue to sleep.

Heinz and Rudi turned up late for Mary the first few times they met her at Bloomsbury House, struggling like we all do to leave the house on time. Once there, the first two days were, largely, about waiting. The three main characters in this part of the story were not the only persecuted Jews arriving in Britain. Day after day they return to the offices, always late for Mary, mostly stuck on the bus. They play football in Hyde Park and, on 21 August, he's still acting like a tourist; taking pictures of green spaces, visiting Tottenham Court Road, talking about how the hell in which his parents were trapped had inevitably changed and scarred his views.

Sometimes he offers updates about the war, which broke out on 3 September. He marked the day with a photo taken in the garden at Windermere Avenue. He and Rudi are wearing gas masks; the caption reads, 'Can I smell war?'

'Yesterday and today,' he writes on 17 October, 'the German air force bombarded England's east coast, especially Firth of Forth.' Sometimes, he includes a newspaper cutting and accompanying photo. A headline above a photo of a coffin and some military, mingling with civilians, reads: 'British Tribute To Dead German Airmen', with the caption: 'RAF men marching in the funeral procession at Edinburgh yesterday of the two German airmen who died of wounds received in the raid on the Firth of Forth on Monday. The coffins were draped with Swastika flags.' It's a common decency of combat loss I have never seen.

Winter arrives and on 2 November Heinz writes: 'English course. Writing. Learning.' Mostly, though, as he settles, he just seems tired. For a second volume of his diaries, still in his first ring binder, he travels to the Home Counties for reasons of work and Blitz. (At one turn, I find a flyer for an event called Old Vienna, at

Café International. There was entertainment in a room dolled up as a traditional Austrian restaurant, with piano recitals, classic dances. The footnote limits the fun. 'If there should be an air-raid warning during the performance, please keep your seats until further instructions are given about shelter. In the unlikely event of your having brought a gas mask with you, we would ask you to be kind enough not to forget to take it with you when you leave.').

He moves beds as follows, four homes in six months – London (21 November 1939 to 26 February 1940); Flint Hall (26 February to 15 April 1940); Earley, Reading (15 April to 21 April 1940); Flint Hall, again (21 April to 2 May 1940); Mortimer, Reading (2 May to 4 May 1940) – but he is nothing if not precise, and faultlessly regular in his writing. Every day. *Every single day*.

And I know that's the point of a diary, but when much of Heinz's life is mundane, waiting in Bloomsbury House, moving to a farm that might employ him, or experiencing events such as on 16 March 1940 – 'I've been appointed first calf boy today' – it's hard to locate the drive to endlessly document.

Maybe it's fascination and a lot of relief. Not boredom, as a cynic could suggest, especially when he draws a diagram of a farm that he works on, labelling cattle trucks and big barns. No, not boredom . . . Rather, he's wide-eyed and grateful, a little touristy and, yes, relieved. Grateful for the country that has taken him in. Wanting to learn about it to fit in as soon as he can and, let's not forget, he's still of school age. This is like a project to him.

A rare moment of dissent arrives at Little Colstrope Farm, near Henley-on-Thames, run by a Mr Keene. It is 8 April 1940 and Heinz is 'getting fed up with work at Keene's'. Rare brevity is found on Sunday, 14 January 1940, as he writes 'Afternoon at Mary's' and nothing else. Fortunate for all of us, perhaps, considering they did share that kiss on the boat from Holland.

But what was it Voltaire said? That 'the way to be a bore is to say everything'? Well, Voltaire was wrong, and didn't understand that the most interesting parts of life lie in its tiny details and, as my grandfather's story unveils itself in epic minutiae, I read it like an orchestra tuning up, playing their tiny parts ever louder and louder, waiting for the symphony to arrive.

Yousef Abdul's English is superb for a sixteen-year-old whose first language is Arabic and who now lives in a German-speaking country, having spent most of his life terrified at home in Baghdad, listening to bombs. He has known nothing other than the twenty-first century. At first, when he was a baby, there was Saddam Hussein. As a toddler he spent years under the booming shock and awe of Western troops, searching for hearts and minds in all the wrong places. As a pre-teen boy, there were the quieter years, at least in the media, as one regime had violently collapsed and another hadn't yet taken its place. That was a period with few foreign troops but lots of violent skirmishes and suicide bombs between different Islamic groups. But those were still the golden years, really, for Yousef, when Isis was still just a river running through Oxford. That all changed in his teens and, just like David in Rava-Ruska in 1914 or Heinz in Vienna in 1939, he was no longer able to stay at home.

I drive to Yousef's flat in Vienna's 13th district. Co-incidentally, it is a five-minute drive from where I used to live in that same city. I know the neighbourhood well. It's suburban and mostly green. A lot of one-way streets for family safety; columns of children walking politely back from school. Trams cruise on overgrown tracks, and I pass a small zoo and mini golf course I remember from my own teens. The supermarkets and cafés and tram stop signs are all the same – untouched in the twenty years since I left. It's a nice place to live and it attracts people who like the fact that it is a nice place to live, and who wouldn't change a thing.

The satnav directs me slightly away from the streets I knew. Left and left and right, up a hill that is a foothill for the mountains that surround the capital. The road is smart, like most of the district. Gated houses and flats with posh balconies neatly laid out with metal furniture and gas barbecues. No clutter, all design. As I carry on to the top of the hill, the pink-orange render chip begins to tip off the outside walls. It's not as nice here as it was at the bottom of the hill. But the children – children with dark skin, girls in headscarves – are happy playing in the long brown grass. They are here. And this is a home for them, so all is, for now, fine. It's hot and most windows are open. I spot an Austrian flag flapping off a balcony. In any other place, you might think this is racist, like a St George's flag flapping from an English balcony. But these blocks are for immigrants only, so maybe it's a family just trying to fit in. Like Adham insisting on paying for my coffee, it's a gesture of self-sufficiency and desperation.

Please, let us. Let us belong.

Yousef greets me at the door. Tufts of stubble and a few wet pimples, he's a boy on the cusp of manhood who has already lived a man's life. He's cool. Calm and softly spoken. But his eyes water a lot when we talk about what has happened to his family, why they are here and how they got here. He leads me into his flat. A small kitchen is off through a doorframe with no door to the right of the only room, which is no bigger than a small lounge in London. Yes, that small. It is where he, his mother and eleven-year-old sister all sleep. Two beds in one room for three people and it's hot – pushing thirty, and it's only mid-May. The home's ramshackle, but not without personalised trinket charm. There's nothing from their home in Iraq, of course, but charity gifts are scattered over the barely-there surface space. A kettle. A television. His sister gets her homework out of a chest of drawers but the drawers don't close properly. One bed has a tired yellow sheet and the other a tired blue one. I don't know who sleeps where, and it's all about making do, but they are here. That is the thing. The only thing. They have been let in and given a room. A little corner of a country without a war has been found for them. They didn't choose Austria for the Wiener Schnitzel.

The journey was hard. In his school project, Yousef describes how they walked from Turkey to Bulgaria, having left Iraq by plane. They couldn't afford anything that would get them somewhere quicker. 'We set off to Bulgaria at one in the morning,' he writes. 'But after five hours – we had been walking in the Bulgarian forest – the police caught us and took our phones and some of our money and hit a lot of boys who were with us and they treated us very badly and said we had to go back to Turkey.' The next night, they tried again and were caught again and people were hit again, so they had to find more money to fly to a different part of Turkey, nearer the sea, where a boat would take them to Greece.

'The next morning we set off by boat,' reads his project, 'but after sailing for 20 minutes, the boat started to leak and water came in. We were so afraid and we could not see anything. There was another behind us, but it sank.' He thanks God for saving them and guiding the ramshackle, leaking vessel to Greece and, from there, via more planes and boats and borders, Yousef, his mother and young sister arrived in Austria.

'We saw this country and we like it,' he tells me. He has aunts in Sweden and Holland. A spread of split family. His mother, whose English seems to be at a level of vague, slightly belated understanding, wants to add something about the sinking boat that took them to Greece. She emphasises that it was more a balloon than a boat.

'Some people sink. Some people are saved. It's luck.' Yousef shrugs, before showing off his teenage years with a tetchy Arabic exchange with his interrupting mum. He looks back at me. 'We wanted safe country, like this.'

His mother had a job with the police. Our drops of shared language are not big enough for specifics, but

73

when I ask why they had to leave Iraq and he mentions Isis – or, rather, 'Daesh' – and how they asked her to do things and she said no, everything is understood. There was a tipping point because you cannot say no to them, but even if they hadn't asked his mother to join them, or whatever it is they wanted her to do, there were explosions all the time. His mother interjects again, but he ignores her this time as he is, of course, a teenager. His father is dead and he wants to assert control. He explains, adamantly, that his family wanted to turn themselves in as that's the legal thing to do, so they darted from police station to police station once arriving in Austria, and were held in cells and holding pens.

'Are you optimistic about staying?'

'I don't know. It's all about luck,' he replies, and it's the saddest thing I've heard. He looks around his home, the tiniest I have ever seen. Smaller than most hotel rooms. He goes to school with Austrians. How welcoming are they? I ask, and he smiles defiantly, says he thinks they will be more welcoming soon. I ask if he feels safer here.

'Yeah!' he answers, loudly, as if it is the daftest question he has heard. 'Because there aren't explosions or Isis, and we have our freedom.'

His mother laughs when I ask if they'll go back. The country where she was born, where she raised two children and belonged, just isn't for her any more. There has always been war, but some wars are worse than others.

'She is so tired from Iraq,' explains Yousef. 'And she

is afraid that they say she has to go back. This is so much better than Iraq.'

I gasp as I leave the flat. Fresh air in my lungs, and the children are still playing in the street. I don't know if Yousef and his family were allowed to stay in Austria.

The summer of 2016 festered with months and months of political bickering that led to many claiming they wanted to emigrate from the country they lived in, while the rest had any burgeoning interest in politics threatened by the way politicians went about their work and played around with lives that weren't their own.

I thought the idea of a referendum was awful. We vote people into positions of power to make decisions and I therefore want political decisions to be made by those in power. It's what should happen in a democracy. If my fuse box at home blows and it looks as though I need to choose between the red wire and a blue wire, I don't make it up and hope for the best. I call an electrician who understands these things far better than I do. The debate around the referendum that summer was much the same. I have not got a clue if it is better or worse economically speaking for Britain to be in or out of a European organisation, and I read newspapers and half of the internet. The millions who don't – as was revealed after the referendum when they asked Google, 'What is the EU?' – know even less.

Yet, the figures thrown at people were complex. It was not sexy. It was complicated. I don't understand the single market. Who outside of actual proper business does? I veered to Remain because everyone has their political sensibility and a newspaper or some affiliation they prefer, and tend to stick to it for their entire lives, following a herd, however well versed in a topic they may be. So I veered towards Remain because of who I am. Because of this family of mine.

Then something unexpected happened.

We had a couple over for dinner and one of them said he was voting Leave. My wife laughed. So closed was our world that we had never met anyone who thought like that before. She laughed a little more and I laughed too, but soon it was very clear that he wasn't joking. He was, he said, going to vote Leave and as he explained why he, as a lifelong left-winger, planned to do so, it made sense. I started to feel tempted too. His reasons focused on EU immigration and the strain it puts on hospitals and schools in areas where thousands settle. Condescending Remain campaigners considered such views racist. But it's surely a fact that if wages in one nation are better for thousands of people than the nation they are from, and if they have a right to move to and work in that nation with the better wages, then they will. Next, they will bring children who take school places. Everyone gets ill and that makes hospitals stretched. This is not an awful thing to say. At the very least, people who believe that and are genuinely worried about their lives and the lives of their children deserve a conversation.

But it was barely discussed. Say the above and Remain campaigners just shouted 'RACIST!' That was the level. The so-called debate on Twitter was blinkered and hypocritical as both sides opted for a monotone of chastising, before accusing their opponents of not being accepting enough of people who are different to them. I live in an area of London with a lot of EU migration. You can tell by the local shops. The accents. The languages in the park. And Ezra will need a school place and I started to think that, if we were out of the EU, because I live somewhere this actually affects, I would stand a better chance of not having to drive a twenty-minute detour to put him in a school we'd been given, but could instead walk up the road to the excellent one a few streets away. That schooling issue was the reason I flirted with the idea of voting Leave.

And when I say flirted, I mean that it would have been nice to have a civilised conversation about how wrong I was, rather than fearing to bring it up in the pub, so hostile had our friends become to anyone who didn't think exactly as they do. I thought about the benefits of stopping mass EU immigration. This would mean, surely, anyone with a more pressing case than an economic one – like Adham, Yousef, Heinz, David – would be more welcome in this country. Because the overall numbers coming in would go down, those men would live. I considered the benefits of stopping mass EU immigration. I considered the benefits of stopping EU immigration. That means I thought about the benefits of stopping immigration.

Farage; Johnson; Gove; the British National Party; UKIP; Ian Botham; the other Leave campaigners whose names I can't remember; Tony Parsons; the vox-pop lot up in Barnsley who said they wanted to Leave because of Islam. Then the people I meet every single day who live near to me, who are wonderful additions to this community and come from Poland; the shock at Jo Cox's death; the fact I love the continent of Europe more than most of Britain and therefore cannot see why we would want to separate; my dislike of cricket, the most Leave of sports; the violent England football fans in Marseilles chanting for Leave; my dislike of uncertainty. My wavering lasted one week and then I voted to Remain.

Of course I did. I can't remember if the final straw was the disappointed tone of my mum's two-word text, 'Oh. Me. x' when I told her I was thinking about Leave – or one of the many racist posters and tweets the Leave campaign unveiled. But, essentially, I could not vote to keep people out when my past has needed so much freedom of movement to get me here in the first place. Some kind of a monster that would make me. A man sitting on his fortune while suffocating everybody who could have a chance like him, because, make no mistake, the people voting for Leave to cut EU immigration are the same people who would want to stop immigration altogether.

Ignore the decent arguments for leaving that were never made in that toxic time and, at the end of the day, it's about humanity and open arms. The way you want the world to see you and how you would like to be welcomed into the world. I enjoy the many languages I hear as I walk to the tube. And there I was, on the verge of giving my backing to racist politicians and ill-thinking people. People who, sometime soon down the line, would want to start talking about deportation. (Across the Atlantic, in Trump's first interview as President-elect, he talked about that very thing.) I was siding with the people who would never have wanted to let my grandfather in – in 1939 there would have been no room. So he would be dead in Austria or a camp in Poland and I would not be here, living on this island that is so absurdly safe compared to most. So safe that its people are able to spend a day laughing at a flotilla of boats on the River Thames, headed by a pop star campaigner and an opportunist from the pub, a week before the biggest vote of their lives.

That summer felt like a cartoon of life, when so much happening around the world was like one of those Renaissance paintings where a central figure is having his guts ripped out. We were a sketch in a newspaper. Then the side I voted for lost.

Chapter 4

The Adriatic coast is dotted with tree-filled islands and tumbledown stone ruins; green and grey the only colours that distract from the panorama of blue filling the sea and cloudless sky. The town of Rovinj, in Croatia, makes its cash from tourists who flock to see such sights, and walk on its cobbled hills splitting time between eating pizza and buying local art. Some wine at three in the afternoon, on the rare days when it pours. Some paradise if you can reach it, as I did, with Rosamund and eighteen-month-old Ezra, just after we'd visited Vienna. Over at one of the town's edges, just below a grand church that seemed to host a wedding a day, nestled on a scraggly lawn, is the bar with the best terrace in town. We sat as Ezra ran and pointed at dogs. A couple of beers of a local sort as we sank back into comfy chairs and considered ourselves decent parents, if Ezra didn't run off the cliff. Around six the sky faded a little. The blues turning black and the horizon rising up tinted with rust. It was sunset, turning those tiny tree-filled islands into darkness and making the ruins disappear. Orange, red and yellow. Nobody needs an Instagram filter when you have real life as artistic as this. Ezra, meanwhile, didn't know what the sun was, so would not understand its need to set. His innocence there was not only enviable, but entirely impossible to maintain. I knew that this view, or similar, had been one of the very last things my great-grandfather David ever saw.

It is fiddly to reach the St Symphorien Military Cemetery by train. The Belgian fields of graves are a fifteen-minute bus ride from Mons station, itself almost an hour from Brussels on the south railway. Once you reach the nearest bus stop, found at Saint-Symphorien Écoles, it is still a ten-minute walk, down narrow country lanes. At least, it being Belgium, the roads are very flat, but dedication is needed to make it up to the gates, beyond the entrance's white steps. A cemetery website's Visiting Information page explains that: 'The location and design of this site makes wheelchair access impossible and can be difficult to access for visitors with limited mobility.' That seems to increasingly rule out most people who would want to visit.

There are 513 soldiers buried there; in an almost even split between the British allies and the German side. Most were killed in August 1914, at the Battle of Mons: a fight notable for being the first major action seen by the British in the war. That was over a hundred years ago now. Some events from then have endured. It was, for instance, when the first traffic light appeared. But others are being forgotten. So much war has happened since the First World War that it is being driven out of school curriculums and, therefore, young minds, only to be replaced by more dramatic, but less deadly – for the soldiers at least – conflict. War like the one that happened between 1914 and 1918, in which the army felt the largest losses, has been replaced by a civilian-threatening global strangulation. Maybe that is why young people still sign up to the armed services – if they knew the losses suffered by their chosen profession during the First World War, they might reconsider.

I don't really know who visits the St Symphorien cemetery any more. Over the last fifty years, as veterans became too frail to drive and far too frail to make a trip by train and bus and foot, the numbers would have dropped off. These aren't those tombs of northern France where coach trips and Year 10 classes go. Nobody holidays in Mons. It is for the bereft to visit the fallen or the survivors to realise how lucky they were; when both of those groups became too old, or died, the fields must have felt even spookier for the remaining visitors. Empty rows of graveyard filled only with silence. I wonder if it will even be there one hundred years from now.

On 4 August 2014, Britain was beaming – putting on the full red, white and blue parade for reports from all the many commemorations to mark the centenary of the outbreak of the so-called Great War (fought by so-called Great Britain). Nowadays, with the internet available to everyone, all the time, even down in the underground, there is no respite from news so, if a positive mood starts, and starts to spread, it will soon prevail. It happened during the Olympics. It happened that August day, too. That day, all the news I read was about the commemoration, and it seemed to make everyone calmer than it should. As if a miserable loss of life was certainly sad but because it happened a hundred years ago, it was unthreatening. Like watching a BBC costume drama which features some death; nobody gets that involved. Something about the finish of a war. White crosses on fresh-mown lawns. Pictures of soldiers from many decades of many different and more recent wars who had lost friends in places they hadn't heard of before they were deployed. Reading about so many minutes of silence the whole day felt hushed, shrouded in a library.

Many of the soldiers of the First World War were boys and between 744,000 and 887,858 of them – someone lost count – perished. In fact, any minute of silence didn't feel good enough. Two minutes feels even worse, like somebody thought a minute was glib but could only hold off noise for another sixty seconds. Maybe, we should have a whole hour of quiet, between eleven and midday each day. It would make us think.

Our Prime Minister at the time, David Cameron, made the headlines that day. He was the one who gambled and lost on our membership of the European Union – but that was still to come. Back then he was just a Conservative leader, liked by the people who like the party's politics, mostly; yet disliked by the people who don't like the party's politics, entirely. At St Symphorien Military Cemetery in Belgium, he was talking about sacrifices made by soldiers during the First World War.

It was a very sensitive speech, as politician's speeches always are, saturated with a gravitas and sympathy so soft it must have been learned. All surface, no feeling, but they are the soundbites that carry. The line Cameron said, rolled out all day among pictures of old soldiers, and worried new recruits looking at the veterans and hoping that they would be allowed to be old one day too, was that those people who had died in that war had done so 'in defence of British values'.

People lapped that up, as if Britishness was a formula to be poured into a beaker, to create the same concoction each time. I have always believed the only thing the British have in common is shared annoyance that sometimes on dropdown menus you scroll down expecting 'United Kingdom' before realising the website has gone with 'Great Britain' so you have to go back up again. That irritation and a passport design is all that the British share – because everybody who lives here is a different shade. Dozens of varied races, but race isn't even the main point. Beneath the skin are brains with millions of pasts; connections that make them impossible to be classified into one cosy whole. A country feels – to me – as graspable as air and yet from that day, up to and after the EU referendum, all around the world, I was in the minority. Over half my country seemed to know exactly what Cameron had meant by 'British values', as that – despite some noise that leaving would be better for the economy, while mentioning the collapse of Greece – is what they voted for on 23 June 2016. In a newspaper article just two months before that speech, he had defined British values as 'belief in freedom, tolerance of others, accepting personal and social responsibility – respecting and upholding rule of law

. . . the things we should try to live by every day . . . To me they're as British as the Union flag, as football, as fish and chips.'

The first part is decent, of course. Nothing that other democracies would not agree with. The second part is the more telling, though. And the more vital given it is specific whereas so much else in the speech is vague. It speaks to a past that is a foreign country, one that many people who voted to leave the EU had dreams of our becoming again one day – and that is weird if your family first arrived in this country less than a hundred years ago, which is many of us.

I don't think I've ever met anyone who fought for the British, and therefore the British values, in the First World War. My connection, on a basic, genetic level, is stronger to the other side. In fact, for Armistice Day in November 2014, I wrote a piece for the *Sunday Times* News Review about this very confusion. The headline? 'I wear a poppy for one of the enemy'. Yes, I sound British. I was born in Surrey. But my great-grandfather was a Galician Jew who fought for the Austro-Hungarian Empire. In essence, with logic, if British troops died for the defence of British values, then David fought against them, which I suppose would make me a little less British than most other people – unless the idea of Britishness is something you absorb immediately with residency, leading to my great-grandfather's son, Heinz, my grandfather, forgetting what it meant to be Austrian like his father as soon as he arrived over here in 1939, which I guess would mean that his father who fought against Britain and therefore against British values, was actually fighting against his own son – and just didn't know it at the time.

I don't feel like I have 'British values' at all, but not because I don't believe in freedom and tolerance, but because I have absolutely no idea what that actually means. I am, of course, British by passport but, more and more, I feel like a collection of foreign countries and people and stories from my past, gathered in a body which happened to be born onto this island of green fields and Friesian cows, Friday night fights and franchised high street shopping lights, and that spends most of its time here, too, but which is more varied than glib categorisation will allow. Those 'British values' the Prime Minister spoke of, thus defining someone by means of country, is a narrow view of what it is like to be alive in this wide-eyed and over-excitable young century; where ever-evolving neighbourhoods of London, New York, Berlin, São Paulo, Beijing and, yes, some other cities in Britain, are populated by interested millennials shaping their own digital world which they share and, each year, has less to do with the demarcated nationality and type of past generations.

Most of my country, though, officially, disagrees. Driving around England ahead of the referendum, through Oxfordshire, Gloucestershire, Sussex and so on, the only thing filling the spaces where migrants and refugees could move into were big Leave posters. To many, nationhood seems to matter more than ever and just as I started enjoying this idea of being the man with no nation, people were vocally and visibly rekindling a passion for flag, sovereignty, royalty, type, race and definition. I've been to eighties discos. I have even won a nineties pub quiz. I know that nostalgia is warm, but a pride in the Union Jack; the raising up of two fingers to foreigners; shouting 'Paki' at people on the street; scribbling swastikas on German cars . . . This is nostalgia from either the Second World War or the 1970s when, I have heard, pretty much everything broke and nobody had lights. The only reason you'd want to return to something like that is if you never experienced it or have forgotten what it was like. After the EU vote, some newspapers ran campaigns to bring back the old blue passport we had before membership, and revert to imperial weights and measures. It becomes harder to argue economic reasons when such old-fashioned stunts take centre stage.

But we, the British, are all so undefinable. Too many people have come from too many different places and been through too much for us to think otherwise. So if the people who died in the First World War – and those soldiers who killed the enemy for Britain – did do so 'in defence of British values', then maybe they were defending a right to be and do whatever you want. Eat pizza while speaking Gaelic and reading Keats, enjoying a brutalist estate with a soundtrack by The Specials, playing darts while voting for UKIP and discovering Buddhism.

But that did not seem to be what Cameron meant by 'British values', certainly not how most people took it. That was why insertion of those very specific details in his newspaper piece was so important. It moved his supporters from ideas onto an era and a stereotype. The

'British values' that Cameron alluded to were interpreted as the sort that you see on old seaside postcards. Everyone's white. We all like bottom humour, have a stiff upper lip and burn too easily in the sun. We love ice-cream when it's raining.

To say I felt removed from that is to hugely understate my distance. Rather, I felt confused. 'British values' in this century are as meaningless as your old Nokia 3210. It works for some, but, frankly, the better parts of the world have moved on to become more complicated, learning from history to expand ideas and become more varied and useful, not stuck happy with something that worked for a long while. Some like to believe you are able to define a landmass by nationality, because it makes everything simple, like lining your books up alphabetically by author name. But it doesn't mean it's very exciting, or easy to let new ones in.

David had only been in Vienna for eleven months when he received his draft notice to start military service for Austro-Hungary, an ally of Germany and enemy of Britain. He was seventeen years old and doing well at school. Decent grades; a boy from the distant countryside settling nicely in the city.

Summers in the Austrian capital are startling, turning its yellow buildings and gargoyled roofs, its wide open spaces and grand waterways, into a sparkling, opulent playground. David would have enjoyed the summer of 1915: swimming in the Danube; walking through the hills that become mountains just beyond the suburbs. But by September that year he was forced to leave an education precious to him, one he had only been afforded because he was a refugee. Bless the rural town, but they do not teach in Rava-Ruska as well as they do in Vienna. Sixty years later in his memoir, he wrote that being called up was the moment his 'life was to take its fateful course'.

He said goodbye to the main squares of his adopted city, which he had learnt about less than a year before and quickly grown to love without a fuss, turning from a boy from the sticks to a teenager in the smoke seamlessly, gratefully. He writes of how he said goodbye to his family and went to the station for army transport to East Galicia – the place he had just had to leave.

David was conscripted at the same time as a friend. 'We both felt depressed,' writes my great-grandfather, '. . . and spoke little during the 20-hour trip, parting company for ever at a railway station in Galicia. The first few days were quite hard and sad.'

My great-grandfather wasn't a soldier. He was a scholar and while he thrived in the move to Vienna, a place with more books than he'd ever known before, it makes sense that he found the second great adjustment of his life, to a military one, significantly harder to get along with. Their long training sessions out east were cold and wet, the barracks they stayed in spartan. He writes how sanitary facilities caused 'great discomfort', and for someone who travelled across Europe, with a large family, to a city that did not welcome Jews with open arms, it says something of the drafting that this is the first time in his memoir that he appears anywhere near discombobulated. He was fed up and found the whole thing 'especially hard and often unbearable', particularly because of 'the bullying drill of the rough-mannered instructors' – quite alien to a man who thrived on academia. One who, reasonably, enjoyed his elders in suits with soft tones – teaching him rather than hitting him.

He was back in Galicia for six weeks, before being posted to a reserve officer school for more combat and terrain training, which he calls 'intensive', with 'difficult' final tests. There were four months of that, then, on 6 April 1916, the front, for what seems to be experience rather than action; travelling through Austria down to South Tirol in northern Italy. Every now and then, he would break to see his family in Vienna. He does not offer any detail other than that. They met a few times. He moved on. His life wasn't his own any more. It belonged to the army, to manoeuvres and training: running with guns and twiddling thumbs, days ticking by before the big event he knew was coming. Some fighting, somewhere. It's the entire arc of *Blackadder Goes Forth*, closer to home for me, and with a less ambiguous ending.

It was down in South Tirol that David saw action. He'd only had brief training, but it was considered enough for combat, in that beautiful and mountainous area of Italy famous for its skiing. David writes that his unit, initially, was successful, but then were moved hundreds of miles to the eastern front, to help the Germans in their effort versus the Russians. The latter were advancing and making breakthroughs. David's war changed.

'Our casualties in dead, wounded and captured were heavy, and were losses which were only slowly made good by eventual resupply of men and materials,' he writes, then talks of positional warfare. Sitting and waiting in no man's land. He says he was out on the eastern front for months, before being moved again, back to South Tirol, via his old homes of Lviv and Vienna – to the front at Isonzo. He did not stop at either of those old neighbourhoods, though I imagined he stared at them as his train went past. Those houses weren't safe for him now, flickering by as he fought the war that made him leave both. It's hard to imagine how conflicted he felt.

Like David in 1915, I also felt sad when I was made to leave Vienna, in 1994, to move back to England. (I am very, very aware of the glibness of this comparison.) Nothing nearly as dramatic has happened to me as happened to him, but that small city sucked us both in because it was, simply, more interesting than anywhere we had lived before. For David, it was the capital of a sprawling empire, rather than a tiny Galician town. For me, it was a city, not a commuter town, where the highlight of any week when you are a teenager is the possibility of a weekend trip to London.

Out in Vienna, over three-and-a-half years, I had become international in my outlook. My friends were Spanish, Austrian, Yemeni, Israeli, British, Sudanese. The first girls I found pretty were called Abeer and Hadeel. I can't remember where they were from, specifically, but it's safe to say they were Middle Eastern.

My school was full of the children of oil families, since Opec was based there. My first girlfriend came from South Africa. I remember breaking up with her at an ice-rink when I saw her smoking a cigarette. So I wasn't cool, but at the very least I was losing the contours of the Surrey mould, embracing the sort of internationalism that inevitably happens at an international school. American pop culture was dominant, certainly more pervasive than British. Bands like Guns'n'Roses or Boyz II Men were more easily accessible during the dawn of MTV than, say, East 17 with their accents and hats, or Take That in their leather. Films were mostly American too, of course. My time in Vienna was the time of *Robin Hood: Prince of Thieves*, when even an American was cast, accent intact, as a rich man from Nottingham. People liked American sports as well. A boom in English football would come, but that was before the Premier League so kids played basketball and followed the NBA. Collected Michael Jordan cards, traded them for Larry Bird. And they loved baseball too, so we talked about The Yankees. Accordingly, accidentally, organically, my clothes changed. In England, a teenage boy will wear a pair of blue jeans and dark green T-shirt, probably from M&S, a stitched picture of an eagle on the front the wildest it would get. Whereas I was into baggy and luminous green jeans, with a Yankees baseball shirt draping way under my knees. It would still be too big for me by the time I went to university.

It was this outfit I picked for a school trip during the first autumn I was back in Surrey. Normally, we were in school uniform. Black trousers. Navy-blue blazer. Red, white, green tie. White shirt. Black shoes. A dark-grey pullover if cold. It was rare for anybody to actually see what anybody was like. This trip, to somewhere I have long forgotten, was miserable – as kids in boring clothes with usual voices teased me for wearing bright green and sounding, to them, like Arnold Schwarzenegger. The only Austrian they knew. My teen accent was a mess. British blended with German, and that pervasive American, into a mix nobody could accurately classify. I couldn't help it, of course. Fashion and accents are an assimilation of what you're exposed to – and I had left Surrey. But do not dare to be different in England, especially when you are young.

Maybe I knew this when I was told we were leaving Vienna. I could remember uniform clothes, uniform ideas and uniform plans. I saw what I had become instead – this absurd hip-hop sports kid who sounded like Hugh Grant playing a Nazi – and was worried how they would treat me back 'home'; whether I could belong again.

So I felt sad about moving, but, also, I think I wanted to go, because I feared becoming even more different from the people at my old school, the people I would inevitably return to at some point. In the end I was back in Surrey for five years before I went to university and became, by the time I left school, exactly like everyone who had always lived there. As international as the A1.

For a country well known for its eccentrics, we really do breed teenagers who hate eccentricities. Maybe it is like that the world over but in Vienna, in my school full of nationalities, everyone could be who they wanted to be, and nobody minded. They teased as teenagers do, about weight, spots, being rubbish at sport. I am not saying these teenagers were perfect. But I don't recall, genuinely, anybody teasing anyone for being different in race or interests. I sat sticking stamps into my album in the middle of the cafeteria and nobody ripped them off the pages. They let people be into the things they were into, and certainly never mentioned a place they might have been born into.

In England, though, intolerance is what I remember of those years I spent back in my own county, before leaving for a university which, at the very least, gave me the option of not hanging out with people I had become friends with before really knowing what a 'Jew nose' was.

I of course hope I would have made a stand if I had known more about my past. But it is hard when you are young – in schools where everyone ends up bullied for some reason, especially if a target is made clear. Kids latch onto tabloid racism as it is the easiest headline to understand. After Trump won the US election, there were reports of schoolchildren lining their bags up in the middle of gymnasiums and telling the Mexicans to get behind the 'wall'. They don't care for the children of children who came from immigrants. Let alone those fresh off the boat. My grandfather didn't feel welcome much of the time when he first arrived, but then his father had fought against his son's adopted country a couple of decades earlier. It was, as ever, a confusing time.

*

The Isonzo is a long river that, with today's borders, splits Slovenia and Italy. These days there are tours of the old battlefields, but I made plans for my visit alone – Mount Rombon and Bay of Trieste; Scot Valley; drive up from Vrtojba a bit – up the valley; Kobarid Museum; Italians have Gorizia; Vrtojba; Karst Plateau; way up Soča (Isonzo); Soča (Isonzo) Valley; consistent wet weather; they stretched to Rombon – bit far?; start at Vrot.

That's what my notebook said.

I stood by the well-kept cemetery in the small town of Vrot, slow trucks rumbling past, hills on the horizon, and tried hard to conjure up emotion. I had read that the war passed through that very town but its memorial was to the Second World War, not my great-grandfather's one, and the notes I made were insultingly brief to his memory, and the memory of others who died.

'So much birdsong it's all you hear. Violins in orchestra chirp on high notes.'

That was it, but up the road, there was more. The actual Isonzo for one, the river so hugged by trees on either side that they reflect off it and make it green. It is beautiful, and still. The war raged up this waterway, at a time when the route's large dam wasn't yet built, but the old stone arch nearby would have been. David would have seen that and, to the desperate, it cannot have seemed like anything but a route to heaven, should you believe in that, and I think, well, what a place to fight a war. Like a bloody punch-up at a pretty wedding – a mix of love and despair. Beauty and violence. Everywhere is water and trees with the only building way up high: a church. But, mostly, it's nature. Thousands of people died here in the twelve battles of Isonzo fought from June 1915 to November 1917, and their bodies will still be underneath, under new tarmac laid down for roads, and the foundations for a restaurant we pass; tempted to stop at its viewing area with tables and parasols, to join the tourists drinking bottles of white wine for lunch. The river has a course mapped out for a kayak race. People carry on. We were carrying on: towards Rovinj.

It was around this river that David was allowed some leave. Some mini-leave, to be precise. It was a busy time in the war and nobody was allowed to go far in case their bodies were needed.

'A short rest-period,' he writes, 'gave me a chance to visit a few places along the Adriatic, which, in contrast to the barren country to the north, appeared romantic and – in which – the sunrises and sunsets remain unforgettable to me . . . These small peaceful excursions were to be the last I was to make as a sighted person.'

At the end of October, the Italians tried to break through to Trieste. This was the ninth offensive on the Isonzo and as such David was called back to the front. There is not much written about this by historians and, in a war of catastrophes, it has become a forgotten skirmish. The Austro-Hungarians were, he writes, expecting the Italians to try and break through, but regardless of planning and anticipation, the battalion and group under his command – numbering sixty – still suffered heavy casualties from the mortar fire and artillery.

'I was badly wounded. A hit by a large mortar shell

fired by Italians wounded me in the left hand, chest and upper jaw and, most seriously, in the face. The latter injury resulted in the immediate loss of my left eye and my right eye was severely damaged through lodgement of a shrapnel splinter.'

He was knocked unconscious, of course, and only significantly later, far away from the front, was he able to receive superficial treatment at a first-aid area. It was clear that wouldn't be enough, so he was moved again by the army to a bigger hospital in Ljubljana, fifty miles away. It was better equipped and run by nuns and specialists who, writes David, were able to provide good treatment for his damaged right eye – such that when his father came to visit he was able to see him. Hazily, he explains, but the familiar face was some solace at least. Both returned to Vienna and, with the shrapnel removed and a course of injections completed, sight in his good eye was restored if not fully, then enough. But he says it was weak and so he had to careful. Little could go wrong, he thought, as a city boy and a scholar in no physical danger from reading books and drinking coffee. He thought he would be able to live within those strictures and therefore with his disability.

But a fall ended those hopes.

What he calls an 'encapsulated sliver of shrapnel' pierced the retina, which in its weakened state had gradually become detached . . . 'I therefore lost my eyesight for ever. It was my fate to live the rest of my life as a blind man.' The last things David saw with any clarity would have been the Isonzo and the Adriatic coast, where he took his leave. There are worse things to have as your final picture. And the birds there, seriously, from Slovenia down, never stop singing. Maybe he can count himself lucky. If he had lost his hearing and kept their song in his head for the rest of his life, there is every chance he would have gone quite mad. Instead, he was able to see the beauty of the water and the trees, how at night the sky turns turquoise and, as you look out to sea, to the tiny islands dotted around, you spot the lights of boats, small homes and hotels, reflecting around each other in a pretty and genteel illumination show.

David was nineteen when he was blinded. One of the fortunate ones, I guess, given that he was allowed another chapter of his life. But he never got to see either of his wives, or either of his sons. He would never see Adolf Hitler, either, or watch man land on the Moon. He would never be able to put a face to any of his grandchildren, like my mum – let alone to me. We did meet, I am told, in 1981, but I wasn't yet one. It was not an event I can remember, but at least now I have travelled to where he was when he lost that most educative of senses – sight; where he was when the light went out and he was, I imagine, just scared.

Chapter 5

The Syrian refugee Noujain Mustaffa has cerebral palsy and made the journey from the Middle East to Germany via boat and wheelchair. The BBC did a short piece on her in September 2015 as she sat, stranded among thousands of others on the shut Hungarian border. The first footage of the sixteen-year-old was of her being carried onto her new continent, since she cannot walk. In a quick interview, she said that she wanted to be an astronaut and that she wanted to find an alien. There was a little bit of giggling, but she didn't seem to be joking. Also, she expressed her wish to meet the Queen and said she learnt English by watching the tackiest of the soaps, *Days of our Lives*. (Improbably, the latter admission led John Oliver to bring back two of her favourite actors for a scene shot especially for her.)

A teenager and therefore a dreamer, her world was made less fanciful as she spent time in detention camps in various European countries, after days on dirt tracks that her sister and others helped pushed her along. 'I am prisoner so, not good,' she said when the BBC next met her. She seemed tired and confused, but ended up in Germany by the side of her brother, who was also seeking asylum. Her parents, though, were still stuck in Turkey, and her Christmas wish was to see them. In another BBC interview, she started to cry as she talked about them, but one thing was clear. This young woman, who has a severe disability, had the willpower to undertake her own odyssey from her embattled, tumbling down homeland; and despite packed boats, tiny rooms and an absent family she somehow managed to remain positive. If not laughing in the face of mad, dramatic-fiction levels of threat, anxiety and danger, then at least not weeping too much either. Before was terrible. This, for now, is just bad. The journalist Fergal Keane, who had met her in Cologne, wrapped up the Christmas segment on Mustafa with, 'There is no telling what she may achieve in the years to come.'

When his own part of the war was over for David, he seemed to be able to ignore the rest of it. There was still a year and a month of fighting until Armistice Day would arrive, but he had now served his shift. Blind and alone, he needed to look after himself and not think about the front or its losses, America's arrival or the Russian Revolution. That can be found in the history books. The story of my great-grandfather in the summer of 1918 did not involve Marne or Siberia or Amiens or the Bolshevik murder of old Tsar Nicholas II. Rather, it involved a journey, by train, back once again to his former home in East Galicia. The place he was forced to leave – only to be forced to revisit it as a conscript, only to leave again, to be herded south to the beauty spot in which he lost his sight. By July 1918, he passed his first state law exams, an achievement which 'strengthened my self-confidence and weakened [the] scepticism and prejudice of the sighted'. That was something he needed to deal with every day.

He wanted a break from studying and the city. He wanted to visit friends and family who, given the rampant uncertainty of the world he had spent twenty years in, might not be there when the next opportunity arose. He writes how living conditions and attitudes back home around Rava-Ruska – 'whether they were orthodox or assimilated, craftsmen, lower middle class or middle class' – seemed the same for Jews, 'in spite of the war and Bolshevist revolution'. But then again the Russian invaders had been distracted by a draining eastern front, which pulled resources away. It still seems mad though, I think, when in the midst of a war that continues to rage nearby, he writes how he 'spent several pleasant, interesting weeks, mostly in Lemberg – the regional capital and cultural centre, which still had the atmosphere of a large city'. Death would have still been all over the headlines, as it is every day these days too, but lives continue. And this was the war before the one of mass aerial bombardment, so more cities and homes were left intact – people feeling relatively free to move about, on foot or ever-thinning horse.

What an image and a shock he must have been to those he had known back home who could not afford to leave in 1914. Perhaps he felt some regret, or possibly even embarrassment. The other Jews had stayed and they were fine. He said so himself. Not that much had changed where he grew up, but he had left with his father and their big well-off family to a foreign city that had not welcomed them, only to return to where he had come from without his sight. David is not one for over-emoting, but that is what reading between the lines is for, and I imagine groups of people behind closed doors talking about the boy who left them, who would have been better off staying put. Of course, those in that part of eastern Europe had further disaster coming, as the Nazis would arrive in a couple of decades, to continue what the Russians had hinted at – digging mass graves for communities to fall into once they had been erased, with no escape for either rich or poor. But, back in 1918, anyone who had stayed could be excused the feeling of relief, while anybody who'd gone only to meet accident or worse, a feeling of great unsettling.

'This was the last time that I was to see my native country,' admits David in his memoir. But he had sixty-six years of largely wealthy life ahead of him – not to mention ever-faster routes to a place under 500 miles from Vienna. At first it seems odd that he never returned to Galicia, but I can only think of this as partly him moving on, partly awkwardness. All conjecture of course – no seance attempted here – and, perhaps, he just didn't like the people back home that much. But sixty-six years is a long time not to visit the place you're from. So I assume it was frustration that kept him distant, and that he had other things to concentrate on now. Points, perhaps, to prove, to those who resented him for leaving but now weren't jealous in the slightest. He therefore had to prove he could make something of himself in the long run, in the new place where he belongs.

He writes how it was the last time that he saw Galicia, even though sight was the one sense he couldn't use there. His memories, in a different part of his memoir, are of the green place where he played with his brother. Those tall trees were bucolic spots to dream in, but now memories were all he had. Come the autumn, he wouldn't be able to see leaves turn brown. He would hear birdsong, but not see the birds. He could talk to those people he'd known as a boy, but not see them age. By not going back after that final visit in 1918, all he had known could be stored in a safe place, keeping his past innocent and not letting it be tainted by sadness felt through his new disability.

But, also, he wasn't a country boy any more. The city had changed him as it does most people from the outside who move there. There is no contact between me and those that I knew at school who stayed in our Surrey towns. What would we talk about? Inertia? Pubs we went to when we were sixteen? Endless nostalgia for a time of life that wasn't even our best. It's an irony, given David's war injury, that the opportunities for him had nevertheless increased now he lived in Vienna rather than Rava-Ruska. After the ninth battle on the Isonzo and the shrapnel that lost him the use of both eyes, he writes in his memoir how he was nineteen, back in the capital, ambitious and energetic, not to mention additional CV boasts of being adaptable, intelligent, with a good capacity for learning. He comes across with the self-belief and salesmanship of a graduate on their third interview stage. A great advantage if you're living without sight in a country still reeling in the biggest war it had faced, a country that was about to become a shrunken, landlocked republic and would, a few years hence, blame you – the Jew – for its predicament.

His eagerness and positivity were key. 'I thus overcame, relatively quickly, the inescapable depressions and feelings of despair.' There were lows. He was human after all, and had sleepless nights, spent alone. And lonely hours ahead of those sleepless nights thinking about how he could see nothing now, maybe remembering the Adriatic, or the battlefield's blood, but mostly thinking, 'how to order my life and to deal with the compassion as well the mistrust and prejudices, of sighted people'. He figured that this could only be achieved were he to study and then be employed in a profession that he found intellectually satisfying and was respected by others.

It must have taken such willpower. The sadness sections are remarkably few. He wanted to be an engineer but says that involves too much practical work for the blind, so rejected it. Next though he landed on and then stuck with law. That was it. Of all subjects, law. A course that takes three years for sighted people in Britain and involves a longer reading list than that of a Barbara Cartland completist. David, though, knew of people like him in Germany. He had heard of somebody called Dr Strehl who set up a school where the blind were able to learn law. So it was not as unprecedented as it could have been. Ambitious, yes. But specialist texts existed, at least, and so he learnt Braille (dusted off with a three-word 'after learning Braille' in the memoir) and was enrolled in a school of law in late 1917 – 'in spite of recommendations of specialists, councillors for the blind and my family – who all tried to dissuade me as they thought that the whole thing was a utopian dream.' (Incidentally, it is thought that no blind barrister practised criminal law in Britain until 2000.)

War support initially treated David well financially. This was mere weeks after he had been relieved of duty – sacrificing his vision for some new chances in life (if you're partial to a bit of life-coach wisdom). He was given a free Braille typewriter, plus a normal one, and several Braille translations of textbooks. He even found an assistant, he says, which no student can afford in 2016. No wonder he managed to forget the war. He was too busy and, anyway, had not been that into it in the first place.

When the war ended Austria was cut to the size it is now. From a landmass similar in size to modern-day Turkey, it was reduced to one just a little larger than Maine. Economic repercussions were felt throughout. Austria was cast adrift from the support structure it had once known, forced to have to live without a wider network of financial dependability. Markets crashed; struggle and panic spread wide. New deals would need to be struck, so the country could support itself, but in the interim, it was all public unrest and painful cuts. Which sounds like something that recently happened in Britain. David writes that these restrictions hit every social standing but were felt worse among war victims. Be it war invalids, the widows or, perhaps, above all orphans, he talks of, 'heavy psychological trauma which led them to question the sense of a war that was lost and sacrifices in health, happiness, economic well-being and career that were made for the Fatherland'.

He too suffered, losing the financial support necessary for his blossoming education. The politically and economically reduced Austria, he explains, was not, at this time, minded or able, considering the privileges he had been used to since being injured, to hand them out as freely as they had been before. 'I had to drastically reduce my standard of living, but I did not give up,' he says. These restrictions seemed only to make him more resolute, knowing that his pension from the war would no longer support him, so he had to study even harder in order to sustain himself financially later on.

In the summer of 1919, he met and fell in love with Tina, his first wife and my great-grandmother. He writes of her in 1975 as though they had just met, as though she hadn't been dead for nearly thirty years. They would live together through so much when everyone else around them was disappearing. 'Her intelligence and warm and lively personality, plus extraordinarily sympathetic understanding of my situation, was an additional motivation for me to intensify my studies so we could marry as soon as possible,' he writes.

She was a full-time secretary, but, just as David was helping his fellow veterans while working to be a lawyer, she gave up her free time too, helping him, and making it possible for her husband-to-be to pass two more exams. They were both making sacrifices. At the end of July 1920, he received his doctorate in law. They married in September, but David leaves behind no detail of the wedding. He is instead occupied with the harder things, as if the wedding was an easy and blissful day he would like to keep private. They opened a tobacconist shop to support themselves, while he strove to find the work he was qualified to do. It was hard for him, partly because his country was so stretched; partly as he had a 'slight handicap', as he calls blindness. It took until autumn 1920 for him to enter any court practice where he, assisted by Tina, worked for fourteen months. Most firms did not even consider him, but 'in spite of disappointments, and because I was an optimist by nature, I was not ready to give up hope'.

Heinz and Rudi are mentioned post-delivery as a vague detail about a happy marriage, in a time when their father devotes substantial space and effort to the Viennese lawyer admissions system. Readers of his memoir know all about that before they know his sons' names. By 1928 he was an independent lawyer, living a fulfilled life. 'I didn't have ambitions to play a role of one of those spectacular defence lawyers,' he says and it feels like the most unnecessary sentence of the lot. He had no need to show off, but had, instead, been able to prove that he could do what he wanted – apart from engineering – and therefore prove if only to himself that leaving Rava-Ruska wasn't the mistake it might have seemed when he went back and saw that most of his friends were fine.

Once, though, in either the late 1920s or the early 1930s – he doesn't specify – David served as defence lawyer in front of a jury. He said that he didn't really have any desire to play the role of the spectacular: waving arms, banging a desk, staring down a jury. He was blind, yes, so maybe that had something to do with it, but, also, he wanted a quiet life. When all up to that point had been noise and pain, he found real happiness in staying at home with his wife and young sons while maintaining a decent career he could be proud of. Contentment not embellishment – and there is nothing to be ashamed of with that. The hurdles that had been hurdled were many and he was happy with a flat race for a bit. But, yes, once, he served in front of the jury. The case was that of an industrial graphic artist, whatever that is, who had been unemployed for several years and sold everything he owned. It was a time of severe economic restraints in Austria, so he had forged coins and notes in order to provide for his family. He was caught and, says David, likely to be found guilty. How he ended up with my great-grandfather as his counsel is not made clear, but the defence put forward was one of 'unavoidable duress'.

Amazingly, his plea was successful and the foreman of the jury so moved by it that he handed the defendant a fifty schilling note to help. ('This time a real one,' jokes David.) My great-grandfather thanks Tina in his memoir and then writes how a newspaper report said he was superb, that his wife thought his 'plea was a masterful example in rhetoric with a visible impression upon the lawyers'.

Satisfaction wasn't found in the fleeting fame of a mention in the press, though. The satisfaction he derived was instead moral, having helped a man – the artist – who was 'in great psychological . . . [and] material need, find a way back as an accepted member of society'. I wonder if, in December 1975, forty-five or so years after the one and only grandstanding case of his life, when he sat down to dictate his memoir, he knew the link he was making there. It sounds like a proxy description. Was he really talking about himself?

He had, after all, found his way back from the brink. Often he's emotionless, flat and understated in his delivery; and his memoir is all the more powerful for that. He, also, was occasionally depressed, but found positivity even though most people didn't want him to become a lawyer. He had returned to his love of music, something he had forgotten for a while, he writes. It's hard to take a piano onto a battlefield or practise scales above rifle fire, but he claims 'a considerable singing voice' which led to a spell at the Vienna Conservatory to train as a concert singer. 'Artistic performance provided many a pleasant hour for me and my audience,' he writes, like an analogue precursor to a boastful pop star's Twitter account.

As a young father I struggle to think up a hobby, let alone perfect it to perform to an audience. My brother-in-law is also a father and yet finds time to go bowling. I know half-a-dozen people who play sports. But they often do that on a Monday night, when there is good TV on Sky Atlantic, and then by Tuesday I am too tired. But I live contentedly, in this absurd job where I am paid to write about the two hobbies I enjoy the most: watching films and listening to music. Perhaps nothing else shows how lucky I am.

David and his family were happy, but he was struggling, quite often, since he couldn't see, and then what we all know is coming happened, which meant that his struggle would double and his children would leave. His positivity is humbling.

Maybe he always expected something bad or difficult to happen, so relentless had his life been up to that point. I live with Rosamund and Ezra in a financially-secure village enclave of London. It has cafés and pubs and deli pastrami shops, and, at the moment, the only worries we have are worries we create for ourselves. This comfort leads to laziness when it comes to others, and the strange truth that looking into history is the privilege of the comfortable, while helping those in trouble has become – and maybe always was – largely the desire and effort of those who are in need too.

In the midst of angst and upheaval, David found time to organise a rally that took place in Vienna in November 1918 to support war-blinded veterans, which led to the formation of the Kriegsopferverband (a very German word) – an organisation that helped old soldiers who couldn't see. I guess some people have fight in them, while others don't. In 2003 there was a big anti-war march in London, and I was so angry about the imminent invasion of Iraq that I nearly went.

In the summer of 2014, a couple of weeks before the birth of my first child, I flew off to Los Angeles to interview Angelina Jolie for the *Sunday Times*. She had been making the film *Unbroken*, about the Second

CHAPTER 5

World War, and we met in an edit suite on a studio lot, where she was finessing the final cut, standing with arms crossed beaming at grand shots of bombers, and talking about her then husband Brad and how he 'loves a shark'. Later I went and sat in an old diner in Hollywood and took stock. I took in everything around me. Red seats; polite and beaming waiters, and a family snapping selfies in a booth. A woman four places to my left was dressed as a tourist attraction – Marilyn Monroe. It did not look like she had plans. I ordered a beer. Trucks of star-spotters with iPhones raised rumbled by, and I asked for a second drink, popping another dollar on the bar for an out of work actor's tip. My life then was at its most casual, carefree, absurd. This would change, partly, with Ezra, but our boy was yet to arrive so I could sit there and just drink. It's possible to sleep off all sorts before you have a child.

I booked an Uber to the airport. I've lost count of the number of times I've been to LA. There was a holiday when I was eight in which I was taken on rides like Star Tours and Jaws by my dad, who was as excited as me, until way past midnight. My mum worried because we walked back in the dark through streets with crimes that we hadn't even heard of in Britain, but it was all fine. My first work trip was in 2006 when I interviewed Owen Wilson just before he tried to kill himself, after which he decided not to do interviews any more. I remember feeling lost, but you can easily feel lost in that city, a succession of interchangeable one-storey homes and vitamin shops that are only reachable by car. My Uber driver was Andreas, and he met me on the corner of Orange and Hawthorn, an intersection cracked by either the fault line or heat.

'Jonathan?'

'Yes.'

'Where will it be to, sir?'

'The airport. Virgin terminal please.'

That was it. I sat back and sent some emails. My feet bulged with the alcohol and sun, so I kicked off my shoes, crossed my legs on the seat. The fabric felt cool for a minute, before clamming up. Barack Obama was in the city. I didn't know this when I sat in the cab, but when the President visits, police close everything. A call was made to Andreas from Uber command. He looked in the mirror.

'They've closed 3rd Street,' he said, frowning.

I grunted. My head was light and I drifted away, lost to warm air that rushed in through open windows, feeling coming back to my feet. I was thinking about jet lag – and how otherworldly it can make you feel.

'All of it, man. All of 3rd Street.'

I was jolted by a sharp stop and reverse, the beginning of a three-point turn. Other cars on whatever street we were on did the same. A dance of direction that makes everyone crawl back to where they came from.

'They've closed 3rd Street, man. All of it,' said Andreas again, patiently.

Like many American cities, LA is a grid; easy to map and easy to close. Think of a painting by Mondrian. A generic one with those black lines, and boxes of colour. Think of 3rd Street as the thickest horizontal line. When it is closed, there is no way to move from the top of the city to the bottom. We were stuck in the top left of a Mondrian painting and Andreas was kind, concerned. I was dazed, relaxed. If I didn't make it to the airport, there was nothing I could do.

I let things go if I feel they are out of my control. Traffic jams or relationships. I only care when I am actively engaged and back then in the car there was little I could do. The police close roads for Obama and don't open them for me. That was it. But Andreas tried to find a new way. I saw yellow route lines on his Google Maps out to the west of the city turn red with congestion the moment we headed towards them. We drove to Beverly Hills, in completely the wrong direction.

'Sorry, man,' said Andreas.

'It's OK.'

Andreas stopped the meter. One hour and twenty minutes into a journey that should have taken forty-five minutes but ended up lasting nearly three hours. Again he told me, again and again, that he was so sorry, and would drive fast and get me to the airport and good luck. He had taken on the burden of something that he had no control over in a way I never think of doing. Unnecessary pressure or fuss was alien to me. Just let it go. Neighbourhoods sped past that I'd never seen before, and I saw two children dance on a corner, laughing at each other with their headphones on. I wondered if they were listening to the same music.

'You over here on business?' asked Andreas. We were spending such a long time in the same car now that it was only right we should get to know each other.

'Yes.'

'What do you do, if you don't mind me asking?'

'I'm a journalist.'

'Oh, cool. What do you do for that?'

'I interview famous people.'

'Interview anyone famous on this trip?' asked Andreas.

'Angelina Jolie.'

'Wow. That's cool, man. Wow. How was she?'

We were on a road I recognised, one that widens with oil derricks on each side and has a subway running through the middle. People who looked like first-, second-, third-generation immigrants waited for a train I never saw and have never taken, on any of my trips. I looked at the time again. The plane was set to take off in thirty-seven minutes. Andreas asked again. He wanted to know about Angelina.

'She's nice, but tough.'

'I'd be scared, man. What did she say? What's she up to?'

'She's made a film called *Unbroken*. It's a biopic about a man called Louis Zamperini who had an amazing life in the Second World War. It looks good.'

'Cool, man. I'll look out for it. Sounds cool.'

Red lights flipped to green and Andreas screeched his tyres on the tarmac. We turned into Airport Boulevard. I clutched my passport tight. If I ran. If I ran . . . I could make it. Perhaps.

'Tell me one thing she said, man.'

'What, now?'

'Go on. Just one thing she said about the movie.'

'OK. She said she wanted to make something positive.'

(Full quote that appeared in the paper: 'It was nice to

bring something positive into the world – to show my own children. I wanted to show them something that's hard to watch in places, but in the end you do, I hope, feel a bit more like, "Well, maybe I can step up and be a better person, too."')

I smirked and rolled my eyes. Grunted a little and giggled. In a rush of trying to make it to the airport I had forgotten I was in America, home of the brave and the upbeat, they say. Andreas was pulling up to the kerb at the terminal. I had under half-an-hour before the plane would leave. He turned to me. First time we were face-to-face.

'What's so funny?'

'I really have to go . . . Thanks so much, though.'

'What's so funny about what she said about being positive?'

'I don't know. It's OK . . . I don't know. I'm British!'

'OK. Well, good luck man. Can I get a good rating?'

'Yes. And I'll email to tell you if I made my flight . . .'

'You'll make the flight, man. Of course you will.'

I did make the flight, incredibly, my name booming from the terminal tannoy, as I did a full whirling dervish through customs, with knocked knees and apologies. Then, I didn't think about my conversation with Andreas for a year. I barely thought about Jolie either, once I'd written up my interview, but then my mum sent a letter, when I started to cobble together what would eventually become this book.

It was a letter sent from David to his son Heinz and as with the diaries of the latter or the memoir of the former, it was a paper heirloom moved from family home to family home while my parents tried out numerous commuter towns in Surrey. Finally, in 2015, as my interest grew from unexpected spark to perceptible flame, my mum brought me this letter.

It feels inappropriate to do anything other than repeat it in full. It is from late 1984, when my grandfather was living in Croydon with his family – having been settled here for forty-five years. Heinz was sixty-one and David was eighty-seven. I was four. Hella is David's name for his second wife, Helene, while Kay is Rudi's (English) second wife. Mama is Tina, whom Heinz and Rudi saw just once more, in England in 1947, after they had fled Vienna.

I fixated on one particular word that he used. The word was *positive*.

Vienna, 9.11.1984

Dear Heinz,

Although it is only a few days since we spoke on the telephone, I was truly pleased to hear that you enjoyed such a successful rest in Cyprus. A journey to a pleasant and beautiful country is an experience in itself, and if, in addition, you achieve the real aim, namely health and recreation, then the experience is to be highly valued. We, unfortunately, will be unable to fulfil our plans this year. As you know, our holiday at Reichenau was planned to last three weeks, but had to be cut short after three days as I was accompanied by such conditions of weakness I had to enter hospital. Our doctor, a splendid, young specialist, insisted on it, and I followed his advice. The excellent treatment lasting six days, however, was of only short-lived benefit.

When, at the beginning of this week, I was walking with my dear Hella to the post office, and on the way back to the bank, to collect some cash (previously I had stayed indoors for some time, while we had some surprisingly cool weather), I experienced repeated and severe attacks of weakness; so much so that I had to stop several times and take nitro-tablets.

Such extreme weakness on such a short walk forced me to go to bed. Naturally, the doctor came and ordered me to stay in bed. As soon as suitable accommodation for us both can be found in a clinic, I have to go there for ten days. This seems to be a prospect for the coming weekend.

Last night was particularly unpleasant, as I was overtaken by a totally novel kind of tiredness and weakness; indeed I feared the end had come. However, a strong cup of coffee and the tender attentions of my dear Hella calmed me somewhat. Let us hope that well-qualified treatment at the clinic will bring a turning-point in my poor condition.

However, do not worry on my account at present.

After Rudi's short stay in Vienna, I developed a real sympathy for Kay, and revised my attitude to Rudi's intention with a view to a genuine life together. I do only wish that the present tensions in his relations with his splendid children will very soon be put right. Until that happens, I would wish that your contacts with him may be even more intensive and cordial than they are already.

I recall a point in your diary which I read during Mama's stay with me in England, and which touched us both deeply. You wrote there that, despite a sunny warm Sunday, you felt out of sorts, because you were alone and bored. That was followed by a sentence which to me is unforgettable: 'My best friend is, after all, my brother Rudi.' May that relationship always remain so.

There is much more which I could add about my life, my relationship with the turbulent world around us in which we have lived for so many years. But that would take too long. I would only wish to add that despite the difficulties occasioned by my fate, I have maintained towards this highly disagreeable world a fairly positive attitude.

The many, often complex problems created by expectations that seem unattainable have not caused incurable despair in me. Indeed, I try to look upon the future of mankind, above all that of the young generation, not totally without hope – in spite of so many depressing aspects.

It is simply that, as a person who feels totally involved, both mentally and psychologically, I regret that age does not allow me to influence, or be involved in influencing more acceptable developments. One would wish that the mental and emotional inertia, so prevalent today (itself the reason for so many ills) may not remain insurmountable and without hope.

Unfortunately, the necessary human examples of

any stature are just nowhere in sight. Too many of those who try to strut the public, political and economic stage are mediocrities . . .

David

David died in Vienna a fortnight after dictating that letter. He had been blind for sixty-seven years, since he was nineteen – a time when I was going to university and worrying about a late outbreak of acne. A line leaps out. The letter is filled with exceptional ones, but my favourite is – 'I would only wish to add that despite the difficulties occasioned by my fate, I have maintained towards this highly disagreeable world a fairly positive attitude.'

In a way it makes me laugh. How extraordinary, in- structive and belittling for us all, myself and the friends I have who shake fists at the world when the train is late, or tweet furiously at Ikea as their checkout queues increase and we have to wait half-an-hour to buy our flatpack occasional table. David struggled through a life completely out of his control. Later, after the war, there was a sense of calm, but it was a calm without sight and full of bad memories. Many people he knew died and his challenges were numerous, but he still felt positive towards the world and, as the letter rolls on, his final recorded thoughts betray a frustration that he didn't achieve enough. He still thought he had something to offer this world. Does everybody feel restless, when they know the end is coming?

I wish I hadn't laughed when Andreas, the Uber driver in LA, suggested that positivity is a good thing. I don't know why I thought it wasn't *British* to agree because blanket nationalistic values don't make much sense to me. Besides, not all people where I live or people in places I visit all over this island are grumpy. They are usually smiling and friendly. They are positive. They want you to have a nice day and if not being drearily cynical is yet another hand-me-down from an ongoing assimilation of American culture and outlook, then good.

Jolie was right. It would be nice to bring something positive into the world to show Ezra. Something to make him feel more like, 'Well, maybe I can step up and be a better person, too.' It's very corny. Of course it is. She's a massive Hollywood campaigner. But she has good sentiments and acts on them. In David's letter he said that 'human examples of any stature are just nowhere in sight. Too many of those who try to strut the public, political and economic stage are mediocrities . . .'

His letter dates from the Ronald Reagan years, so it's unfathomable what he would have made of Trump, but not all celebrities who dabble in politics do so for their brand. Jolie talked to me at length, and with pride, about her frequent, challenging, pretty-much-full-on job for the UNHCR, fixing me with a deep, incredulous stare while discussing new, shocking refugee figures that showed more people were displaced in 2014 than at any time since the Second World War.

David would admire her, I think. He would have to, really, given that career politicians rarely speak with conviction about anything these days, lest constituents be angered and then not vote for them at the next election. He can't look for leadership there. The letter mentions the 'future of mankind' and a hope in the 'young generation'. Have all the generations since let him down? The world has never felt as fraught as it does now. I spoke to a colleague in his mid-fifties, two decades older than me, about other periods of his life that felt as untethered as today. He said the seventies were strange with blackouts and a nuclear threat. Then the eighties had AIDS. But, either way, he agreed: these are frantic years.

I live in a world where I am constantly looking for exits. I have been ever since the Paris attacks in November 2015. I look for exits in restaurants and pubs; on the train. If they come for me and I am there and my family is there, I need to know how to get out. I was in Paris the week after the Nice murders, sitting on the grass in Place des Vosges. It is a square park with four exits and I thought, do I sit in the middle as they will come from outside – and that means there will be people between me and them, giving enough time to find a way out? Or do I choose one exit and sit by that, assuming they only arrive via one gate? That gives me a quarter chance and better odds, and this is the world I live in. I don't think it's what David expected to happen.

At the time of writing, I am thirty-six. I have followed a path and the path has rarely been diverted. By the time David turned thirty-six he had been a refugee, a soldier, a blind man, a lawyer, a husband and a father of two. And he had started to realise that his new home was under threat from a politics that hated him. His sons' flight and his own spell in a concentration camp awaited him. So I find it remarkable that he calls the world 'highly disagreeable'. There are stronger words available.

We all have disappointments. A job that goes to someone else. The novel you wrote that just won't be published. The third flunk of an expensive driving test. Life is work and, yet, adults give up too easily. A fully developed brain is used as an excuse for inaction. We're better when we have barely spent any time on this planet. When I saw Ezra as a baby constantly, instinctively, strive for improvement, I would think our inaction was regressive. Each day for him was a near-blank canvas that he will find a way to fill, and some days will be prettier than others. Some may be almost entirely upsetting. (We get to hear about them loudly.) Adulthood brings complexities that mean we can't start each morning afresh, as he (nearly) can, but there is always some space to change. Something we failed at, which we may not fail at again.

My great-grandfather was blind and persecuted, yet lived until old age and remained positive about this world. It's like surviving a fatal car crash and telling your children that driving is good. My baby couldn't crawl for months, but learnt how to move, and he smiled all the time. Jolie never needs to work again, but she wants to help people and so she does. Then there is Noujain Mustaffa.

Somewhere a little lazier is me and most other people. I do not believe in the afterlife and hope there isn't one, because if David is up there he would despair. Millions are on the run from danger like his family were, barbarism back in the headlines (if it ever went away) and, mostly, we nearly go on marches.

Somewhere seemingly random in his diaries, my grand-father includes sheet music for a song called 'Katia'. It is the only music he includes in any volume. I didn't know it, but Google does and after digging around on the internet, I find what I convince myself must be the correct song.

It's actually called 'Katia (Il Peut Neiger)' and the version I find is sung by one Leo Marjane. It's pretty, scratchy, with ample violins, and since I have no idea what Marjane is singing about, it turns into the scene from *The Shawshank Redemption*, where inmates hear an aria from *The Marriage of Figaro* and are transported not by words, but music; as music shouldn't be studied, it should be natural and felt, so it can take you some place away from your brain. Music is, after all, the second best thing in the world after love and, as I carry on with Heinz's diary, I play 'Katia (Il Peut Neiger)' over-and-over again.

While doing so, I felt more connected to him than ever before, even more so than when I look at a photo of us on a sofa – I'm playing with a Spider-Man motor-bike and he's smiling, his arm around me. Because back then I was four, and I can't remember anything. All I remember was when he died, around Christmas 1985, and Mum came home from hospital. I heard the front door open and raced downstairs with such speed I was in time to see it close. It's all I recall from the eighties, apart from Diego Maradona, cutting my knee, getting an activity folder from a bank, watching *Bambi*, rolling down a hill, seeing a removal man spit out coffee, buying a Panini sticker album and going on holiday to Spain, where my parents ordered too many cakes. Mum is a small woman, but she seemed smaller that night, shrunk by the flying away of friendly ghosts.

In my mind, then, Heinz and I didn't properly meet until I read his diaries, and discovered what he used to enjoy, reliving a short section of his eventful if too brief life. His sense of humour and eye for detail stand out, but I never felt as in awe as when I played that song 'Katia (Il Peut Neiger)' on my headphones while reading his entry on 23 September 1940. It was a Monday night in Mortimer near Reading and Heinz was in a philosophical mood.

He compares human beings to atoms. Man has, he argues, innermost parts like a proton, which are always positive, but electrons – 'outer signs of character' – are split as in an atom, into positive and negative. There is more theory, metaphor, how, with negative being attracted to positive, man has a propensity for wrong, but he concludes, forty-four years before the letter that his father David sent him, that, 'I believe this good part in every human being will lead to a better world . . . I believe that man is good, in his innermost, sometimes hidden part.'

I read on, 'Katia (Il Peut Neiger)' stopping only to start again and I keep it on, umpteen times in a row even though I was starting to lose my mind.

When we are starting to build this better world [continued my grandfather, on that Monday], we must not believe we will succeed in doing it quickly . . . We will have to bring man up to a high standard of morale which will make him realise that he is and has to be good. A hard, but possible job. As Hitler has already proved that it is possible to bring man up to a certain standard; in his particular case the lowest standard one can think of . . . He has educated a new German generation to brutality, malevolence, ruthlessness and hatred . . . Why should we not be able to educate the next generation and the following ones step-by-step to this high standard of morale which is to give us the foundation for our new and better world? Hitler taught them to hate, we shall teach them to love, that all men are equal and have equal rights . . .

Turns out that despite what had happened to him, he was positive too. Four days later, though, on Friday, 27 September 1940, Heinz wrote: 'I really feel too lazy to write in this blooming diary.' And he has never sounded so human.

Chapter 6

I met David once, in a garden in Windlesham, Surrey. I don't remember. It was 1981 and I wasn't even one, a baby on a floral patio chair holding onto an armrest as I couldn't support myself. My sister Claire is on the same chair, sitting straight, eyes fixed firmly ahead with a look that begs, please, please get on with it, my brother is wriggling. My auntie Fiona offers my shoulder a helping hand, to prop me up in case I fall, while my mum looks on. She wore a red jumpsuit that day, with her hair in a perm and, while it takes someone extraordinary to steal attention from an outfit like that, there are two men in the photo than manage just that. First, in dark glasses and a spotty tie is David. His body sags with age and history. He hadn't seen a thing for sixty-five years and knew his second wife Helene, to his right, only through his other senses. We were just foreign accents and gurgling. But he's smiling. That day, for him, was close to bliss, I guess. All that he had been through and this bunch, his family, were safe in England's greenest and cutest county. It wasn't even like we had to make do in the West Midlands.

The second man able to upstage the jumpsuit is Heinz.

He stands behind his father, a hand on his stepmother's shoulder. (Thanks, that says to me, for helping the old man out after the war.) Heinz is glowing. He looks tanned in a way nobody in England did before tanning salons, and so casually posed – with a slightly dropped left shoulder – that he cannot help but betray a life of eventual satisfaction. Such a vacuum formed when he died. He looks lovingly at the person taking the photo, Marion, his second wife after his first, my grandmother Mary, passed away before I was born. In less than five years after the photo was taken, both Heinz and David would be dead, leaving a gap in the image, between the English on the right and Helene on the left; a foreigner. It was a divide that grew wider for a while, before we moved to Vienna and tightened family ties. Windlesham is all leaves, people carriers and garden centres. In many ways, an incredibly pleasurable and easy part of the country and such victory, I think, for Heinz – who came over to this country as a refugee and was baffled by much that he experienced. A lot of people were racist to him because, being Austrian, they probably thought he was German. Plenty more did not trust him as he was a Jew. To begin with, his parents were either in occupied Austria or held as prisoners in a concentration camp. And yet there we are, in Windlesham – in a constituency that returned more votes for UKIP than any other party in the 2014 European Parliamentary Elections. They took 32 per cent of the vote. There are people in Windlesham who don't like immigrants and refugees and so I wonder who lives in that house now. Who sits in the garden where a refugee stood proudly in 1981 with his refugee father?

*

In one of the very earliest telegrams that Tina sent her son – which arrived in England the day before he did – she wrote: 'I am convinced that it will only take a few days for you to become enthusiastic about the new and wonderful things you are going to experience.' He took her words to heart. On Sunday, 24 November 1940, Heinz had what he called 'one of the most remarkable journeys of my life'. It started in Richmond and ended on a train to Basingstoke. How strange, I think, to apply the word 'remarkable' to the Richmond to Basingstoke line. Especially when you've recently taken a train to England from Nazi-occupied Vienna, via Nazi Germany and an antagonistic border guard.

He writes that the journey began at 7.30 p.m., when the sky was full of 'banging and lighting of the guns'. His first train was to Reading, supposedly departing at 7.38 p.m., arriving in the Berkshire town at 8.43 p.m. The platform was still empty at 8.10 p.m. Passengers were told they would need to change trains at Twickenham. This is half the detail that he provides. When he finally makes it to Twickenham, the station is packed. Ninety per cent soldiers. Guns are still blazing away at German planes high above the capital. Searchlights swoop. Planes soar. And, no surprises here, the train doesn't appear, so Heinz thinks anxiously of the 9.35 p.m. from Reading that goes to the station closest to his home: 'I hope it will be late, as usual.' Eventually he boards at Twickenham. In his diary he names the Home Counties villages and towns that the train creeps by, places I knew when growing up. At 9.50 p.m., he passes Sunningdale, where we had our family dentist, Mr Parker. Then at 10.10 p.m., Bracknell, home to the greatest adventure pool in the area, Coral Reef. (Three slides! Fast rapids! A pirate ship with water-jet cannons where school gossip claimed they once arrested a sex offender . . .)

On that Sunday in November 1940, Heinz just thought about getting home; sleepiness turned to neurosis and he smoked five cigarettes in two hours. When he finally reached Reading he ran to the platform and, brilliantly, being Britain, the 9.35 p.m. was still to leave, at 10.40 p.m. So far just a story of an average commute, but Heinz had really built this up. Something truly remarkable must be about to happen. The train was pitch-black so, partly because he was worried and partly because he often spoke to people on public transport, he checked with a man in his carriage if it was indeed the right train to Basingstoke. He could make out that the man was in uniform. The man said it was the right train. Heinz continued.

'You are going to Salisbury, aren't you?'

'Yes'

'You are tall and fair-haired?'

'Yes'

'Well, don't think I am funny or queer, but I have met you on this train twelve weeks ago. We were in the same compartment . . .'

Heinz writes how he recognised the man from his voice alone, adding he was 'dumb with surprise'.

That was what was remarkable about the journey.

A bit of war at the start perhaps added to the sense of

occasion. But mostly the remarkable event of a journey from Richmond to Basingstoke was that he was on the train with someone he had been on a train with before, on a route both men often took.

I turned back the page to see if there was something I missed.

There was nothing and, it seems, to me, it was pretty much the least eventful thing that had happened to Heinz since coming to the country. But perhaps he was just trying to please his mother. He was being enthusiastic about his new country and trying to fit in so residents would not think him different from the rest. Over a year after Tina sent that telegram, he's still taking her words to heart. Be thrilled, came the message from Austria. Be so thrilled that recognising a man on the train that you take most weeks is up there with the most extraordinary things ever to have happened to you. Be happy and grateful and they will let you belong.

His diaries covering the years 1940 and 1941 are a blow-by-blow account of the life of a very recent refugee. Much of the content is work, searching for work, leaving work, having arguments with employers, meeting people who cannot pronounce his name so give him nicknames, comments about the weather turning very cold and wet, and, relatively soon after arriving, some routine and the quiet he was longing for, which his parents wanted for him, and for which he too was thankful. His sentences and snippets become the phrases of anyone who lives in Britain, of any generation; frequently, delightfully mundane. It is rare that he sounds like anything other than a local. Some newcomers stay in near-ghettos and rarely interact with people who aren't like them, but others – like my grandfather – seek to abandon that difference as soon as they can. It is the aim of most. Take the Syrians who have come over this decade. Will people know them as Syrian in thirty years? By then they will have been to mixed-nationality schools and applied for the same English-speaking jobs, and will use phrases like the following, that my grand-father discovered very early on: 'I am getting used to the place'; 'Enjoyed myself immensely driving a tractor this morning'; 'An eventless Christmas day. A feeble party tonight at my landlady's daughter's'; 'A most uneventful, routine start of the year'; 'Nothing of importance'; 'All quiet on all fronts'; 'If am not lucky, then I don't know who is'; 'I am bored stiff with myself'; 'I am perfectly comfortable and, in consequence, lazy'.

My mum says that when her friends met her father, he was just another Englishman to them. He didn't have an accent at all. People did not know where he was really from.

But back in those early days in his new country, as the war lingers on, hints of his past and his preoccupations do drop by. Not with mentions of his parents who, peculiarly, hardly ever come up – especially peculiar given that his father had been through similar cross-continent upheaval at a similar age – but with the inclusion of so many basic facts about the war that certain entries are more encyclopaedia than rumination.

This is stranger when you think how unlikely it was anybody would read these diaries after he wrote them. I know that Heinz himself did, because of an annotation in a margin from 1971 that reads 'What a joke!' next to a passage where his young self wrote optimistically about a mooted Franco-British union. Also, I know someone read them to David, since he mentioned them in the letter that he wrote two weeks before he died. But other than those men, it took me the best chunk of a century to even pick them up, despite my quiet interest in my interesting past. His children didn't know about them until after he died and have skimmed through them at most. I assume Mary did too, and I have been told that Marion has been through parts, but he was not to know in the 1940s that he would marry one, let alone two women who, out of curiosity and care, would want to discover his life before they knew him.

In that way, the entries – whether historical or personal – feel like Facebook updates, but without any Friends. Status Updates From a Recent Refugee sounds like a column for the *Guardian*, but many of the blows and trials he writes about would have been softened by people commenting that he was OK, really, or they were going through a similar ordeal, offering some Likes. The only echo coming if he read the diary back to himself and, in this lonely period of his new life, it is clear the vast problematic swamp of the world had become too much for him to ignore. He writes much more about current affairs than any personal woes – and he writes with a desperation, which begins to come to the fore on 17 June 1940.

'Since 1 o'clock today,' he writes, 'my nerves are wholly wrecked and I am quite unable to think or come to any conclusion as to what is going to happen . . . I have lost any hope or confidence: France has given in! Is there any way out? What will happen to the world? To mankind? To us poor refugees?'

Then, four days later, when General de Gaulle signed the armistice with Nazi Germany, Heinz just writes that every word uttered about anything other than that – that day – and I guess he means uttered about himself, is 'superfluous'. That night he is so downbeat and depressed he sleeps through two air raid warnings and – as 1940 rolls on and he marks the first anniversary of his arrival in Britain – the journey from Vienna via Frankfurt and Cologne, with its tear-wet farewell and real threat at the border, so clearly becomes the end of that first life of his; with the new one a task he has to overcome and turn into an opportunity, if given the chance.

The tedious registration process in Bloomsbury House; sightseeing, cinema trips, farming, endless, endless farming (at school, in the big city, he had studied anything but farming); the confusion with this country's customs that he wants to understand, from the way we use cutlery to how people don't get classical music; continuous, often doomed thoughts of war, parents that he barely hears from and perhaps from fear or even guilt doesn't talk about . . . Most of the time, in his diary, he seems to be desperately trying to move on from a place he knew and which kicked him out. Everything is about him trying hard to assimilate and, as such, the disproportionate excitement he felt on a train trip from Richmond to Basingstoke acts as another bookend. From then on, rare is the moment that he is an excited schoolboy on a trip; rather, more normally, an emotional, over-thinking, intelligent, worldly teen barking at the unsettled world.

His first twelve months in Britain packed two acts of plot into one young man and – by 3 September 1940 – a year after the signed start of the Second World War, Heinz is on his third act: when the protagonist becomes who they are. He is in a field with a colleague. It was, he writes, a bright and sunny day and the war felt far away. He turns to this unnamed co-worker and says, 'All around is nature . . . You see nothing but fields, woods, brooks, cottages, men, working in fields just like us . . . peacefully and quietly. We all seem to feel that the slightest noise would disturb this calmness which fills the air. Can you believe that we are at war?'

At that point, a military aircraft flew over the field and Heinz wonders what the effect of that constant exposure to war hardware, 'proof of the barbarism that reigns over our world today', would have on 'kids of our time from the ages of three to eight years . . .' He continues, 'They hear aeroplanes and bombs each minute as if it is a matter of course. Is this not most unnatural? We can be proud of ourselves!' Sarcasm, it appears, is a thing that survives even the most miserable of thoughts. A key to making it through anything, and the world then was going through everything. He writes of Richmond and Kew and the severe bombing that they suffered – 'fifteen houses collapsed and are a heap of rubble. Bomb holes, half-broken-down houses, gardens, buildings everywhere. Above all, sixty per cent of windows at Kew are broken. The famous glasshouse in the garden is left without glass.' London, he writes, 'was lit up like a torch' – and his own mind seems to flicker between raging fire and ember. A person, I think, made up entirely of raw feelings, who is trying to keep them hidden because that is what British people do.

On Thursday, 6 March 1941, Heinz considered joining the RAF. How odd. He had been in the country for less than two years. He was from Austria who were, since they had been annexed by Nazi Germany, the enemy. I thought British soldiers died in the defence of British values. How would Heinz know what that meant? His father fought against Britain in the earlier war and they share a country, so must he too share values? Or are borders a line not a rule? I wonder.

The fear my grandfather had about joining the air force was if the Nazis found what he had done and who he was fighting for, they would round up his parents and retaliate against them. They were stuck in Nazi territory. The hope he had about the RAF was that it wasn't farming. He went into a recruiting office in Reading, and they told him that his parents would be fine. Foreigners were allowed to join and the Nazis won't know anything about his new affiliation unless he was shot down in his plane and captured and, said the man behind the desk, smiling, 'You don't look the sort of fellow to be captured easily.'

The officer thought that he was signing up on the spot – and made him fill out forms there and then. Heinz backtracked a bit, saying he needed the permission of friends looking after him, not to mention permits that he needed to sign off and work notices that must be served. It was a real dilemma, he writes, but, soon, in fact, just four days later, he says he doesn't think he will join the RAF after all. A conversation with Rudi stopped him and, though the detail is non-existent, it can be fairly assumed he feared the violent effect on his mother and father or, perhaps, their reaction. Is it really worth it, they would think, going to the effort of leaving your own country only to go to a recruitment office and sign up for the armed services a year and a bit later? In order to risk being killed by those who would have killed you anyway, in the comfort of your own street or a camp somewhere nearby? David had no choice. He was forced to fight for Austro-Hungary in the First World War. I imagine he would have been furious if his son had volunteered and then was blinded or worse. David's sacrifices were not made for his son to become a soldier and a statistic, even if there is inevitably another reason for Heinz wanting to join, even if he never expressly says so much. By being in the British armed forces, he would be fighting against the Nazi army and their allies who were engaged in or at best ignoring a systematic extermination of the Jews. There were, to me, two reasons that he walked into the recruitment office that day. One, to feel more British and assimilate further into the crowd. Two, to fight back. But, despite such strong convictions, he said no. The loss would not have been worth it.

And, besides, farming is not that bad, despite telegrams from David and Tina to Heinz and Rudi early on in their stay in England expressing shock that these city boys might not be able to find a technical college or employment. The problem, went David's argument, with agricultural courses was that his sons grew up in the city so weren't used to the country life, forgetting he himself did the same – albeit the other way around and that people can change just like that. 'We'll swing it somehow, as you – dear Heinzerl – used to say so strikingly,' wrote David. Mention is made of an uncle over in America, who is willing to offer $20 a month to make their expensive technical education possible, since such schooling will lead to a more secure future than spending years on a field.

'Besides,' the telegrams continue, 'you don't have proper clothing, shoes, or underwear necessary for a stay in the countryside. I hope to receive pleasant news from you shortly, not about a barn, however, but rather about technical school.'

I am not sure what the difference is between city and country underwear, but it didn't matter. Refugees can't be choosers and at least their quicker route into the (agricultural) school offered financial independence and decent accommodation. It would surely have pleased David greatly that Heinz wound up as managing director of a timber company, and subsequently the chairman, with a salary decent enough to send both daughters to private school. He would have been pleased and, also, amused – the timber business at Heinz's level was a fine mix of country and city. He worked out of Deptford and dealt with lots of wood – having risen to the top of what this country is able to offer, starting from a refugee's default position of nothing, with no formal education past sixteen. I wonder what the people who thought we had too many Jews coming over in the 1930s would say to his life. I wonder what arriving Syrians, Poles, Nigerians, Turks, Iraqis – the list goes on – will go on to do with their time here.

Reading on, however, other reasons for not joining the RAF become, if not a primary factor, then at least a bugbear. The nag you won't admit in public but becomes a deciding factor nevertheless. Very simply, my grandfather had some issues with the English. On 11 March, just after he has decided that signing up wasn't going to happen, he is 'in a rage . . . at those blasted, damned uncivilised people' because music he was enjoying on the radio was shut off early. He also says, 'people know surprisingly little about music in this country', which seems fair given the era, given that Austria's classical output is unparalleled, even if a contemporary countryman of his would struggle with that claim nowadays, what with the comparative talents of PJ Harvey and DJ Ötzi.

Other – significantly more serious – problems infuriated him about the English. At one of his farms in Berkshire he strikes up a friendship with a man called Claude. 'Very nice, but a proper type,' writes Heinz.

He has, like every Englishman, got the right to vote, but he does not, because politics don't interest him. He does not read a paper! Why? Because outside his job, his family, his hobby nothing interests him. By no means is he doing the duty of a citizen of a democratic country – that is, help ruling it! An average Englishman. He would damned soon protest if his right to vote was taken away from him, but now that he's got it, it's of no interest to him.

Then there is the establishment. As a lonely refugee, he spends his time and money on the arts. Cinemas, mostly, and classical music. But options on Sundays, one of his few days off, are limited because of archaic licensing laws. This leads to a rant.

'There's some stupidity going on in this country,' he vents. 'While cinemas, pubs and concerts are open on Sundays, a bill to open shows and theatres – too – was defeated in the House by 144–136 votes; most claiming religious grounds for their stupid, dusty, daft, old-fashioned Victorian attitude and views.'

These are not the moans of an ungrateful refugee. In fact, by going on walks, to pubs and even trying to talk to people on trains (therefore misjudging the national psyche entirely, admittedly), Heinz was trying very hard to fit in and be accepted. All his gripes about music, politics and the establishment strike me as very reasonable. He wanted to belong here, yet there were things that he couldn't understand and those issues bothered him into thinking that, maybe, he would never belong. Maybe, he would always be an outsider. He seems to think similarly to how I do now. It's too much to say I hate this country, but I love it less than I used to. I adore so much all that goes on here and is created here, but recently, to me, Britain has been a good meal spoilt by hidden and rotten parts; it seems little my grand-father complained about has particularly changed. Those 'stupid, dusty, daft, old-fashioned Victorian attitude and views' have hardly left the Houses of Parliament. That is what strikes me most. We're a country that often shuts its ears off to the greatest arts; and we are even lazier at politics.

Claude is a 1940s representative of the 28 per cent of this country who didn't vote in the EU Referendum. We are allowed that lack of involvement, because we are successful and comfortable – but it doesn't make me proud. It is shameful; how awful, really, when you think how much was sacrificed by my ancestors to ensure Heinz made it to England. And yet, these days, I question this country's values and plenty of its population too.

So, perhaps my grandfather didn't want to risk his life for the RAF, because he didn't feel that this was a country worth dying for, despite its being in direct conflict with his family's persecutors. There were too many things that hadn't been welcoming.

There is an entry from his diary on 7 December 1941, which reads, 'I don't know if I shall ever be able to find a woman in this country completely likeable. They certainly are absolutely crazy . . . And, today brought another example of the state of mind in which I've found most English women to be.'

His reasoning appears peculiar to begin with. He and Rudi are sitting in one of the many farmhouses they worked in after coming to Britain, with some people they worked for and lodge with. Together, they listen to the radio. The discussion turns to the wedding of the Belgian monarch, King Leopold III, some months earlier about which – Heinz claims patronisingly and cheekily

– someone called Mrs Beale 'knows a particularly ridiculous yarn which amounts to the fact (supposed fact) that King Leopold died in 1935 with his wife. And this man is only a double put up by the Nazis and ever since kept under their thumb!'

He is incredulous. But hardly with a decent cause to dismiss every English woman. It is just idle gossip. People say things like that on Twitter all the time. The conversation in the farmhouse, though, hurtles on. Heinz was further annoyed by something Mrs Beale says about the Japanese; specifically how they could never be any danger to her.

'Do you feel superior to the Japanese?' asks my grandfather.

He expected a simple response, but his question led to an outburst of abuse.

'Most certainly I do!' she blurts out like an erupting pipe after her bile could not be contained any longer. 'I feel superior to any foreigner. I am a Britisher!'

And there we go. The ability of our islanders to talk up a shrunken empire. The room sat dumbfounded – with Rudi pushing his plate away and saying Mrs Beale had no reason for saying what she had. That got her going again, ranting on and on and on about superiority, how some people, those in the same room as her, had no consideration of her country's glistening past and great history, and how they were too young to know anything anyway. They did not know anything because she had experienced everything. It is a small scene for an allegorical play about Brexit. The punch-line is that Mrs Beale claimed that Japan was no threat

David and Tina, Vienna

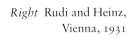

Right Rudi and Heinz,
Vienna, 1931

Below Family portrait, 1931

Above left Heinz, David and Rudi, 1935

Above Heinz and David at home, 1938

Staats-Realgymnaſium in Wien 1. Bezirk

Stubenbaſtei 6—8

Jahres-Bericht

über das

66. Schuljahr 1937/38

Wien 1938
Jm Selbſtverlag des Staats-Realgymnaſiums im 1. Bezirk

Left Heinz's school report, 1938

Left Heinz, Vienna 1938

Above Tina and David in the flat at
14 Hohlweggasse, 1938

Below Heinz (fourth from right) at
the Jewish school he was moved to,
the Zwi-Perez-Chajes Schule, 1939

Sunday afternoons in Richmond, February 1940

FR/C 7.

Foreign Relations Department,
Red Cross & St. John War Organisation.
The Lord Chamberlain's Office,
St. James's Palace, S.W.1.
Tel:
Whitehall 3007.   Date as postmark.

In answer to your communication of 9th May, 1941
we will take all possible steps to trace your
relatives/friends.

We may have to communicate with a good many
offices here and abroad. Postal communications
are often greatly delayed, so you must not expect
a reply for a considerable time.

Sympathising with your anxiety.

S.J. WARNER,
Deputy Director.

25)

FILMS SEEN IN THIS PERIOD

TITLE	STAR MALE	FEMALE	PLACE	TIME	THEME	Co.P.	POINTS
GULLIVER'S TRAVELS	—	—	Brobdignag	1669	Fairy Tale Cartoon	U.S.	2
KNIGHTS OF THE RANGE	—	Jean Parker	U.S.	19th temp.	Cowboys D	1.S.	3
HIRED WIFE	Bryan Aherne	Rosalind Russell Virginia Bruce	U.S.	Contemp.	Society C	U.S.	4
TOOTH TO KARANDA	A. Birk Ford H. Hoscowich	Lili Seste	Africa	Contemp.	Ridiculfication D	U.S.	2
NICE AFFAIR	R. Boyer	Irene Dunne	France U.S.	contemp.	Nice D	U.S.	4
CRIME IN THE AIR	—	—	U.S.	Contemp.	Detect. C.D.	U.S.	3
THE GREAT DICTATOR	Ch. Chaplin Jack Oakie H. Hoscowich	Paulette Goddard	Tomania	1918–1938	Polit. Satire C.D.	U.S.	7
VIRGINIA CITY	Randolph Scott Errol Flynn Humphrey Bogart	Miriam Hopkins	U.S.	1865	Civil War D	U.S.	4
ROBIN HOOD	Errol Flynn Basil Rathbone Ian Hunter	Olivia de Havilland Robert Donat	E	11..	R.H. Adventures D	U.S.	5
HENRY STEPS OUT	—	—	E	contemp.	M.D. up C	E	0
NEW MOON	Nelson Eddy	J. Mc Donald	U.S.	1789–92	Floodtime M.C.	U.C.	2
QUEEN O.T. MOB	Ralph Bellamy	—	U.S.	Contemp.	Detect. D.	U.S.	3
FREEDOM RADIO	Clive Brook Jack Farr	Diana Wynyard	Germany	1938/39	Anti-Nazi D	E	2
QUEEN O.T. YUKON	Ch. Bickford	—	Alaska	18..	Gold Alaska D	U.S.	2
THIEF OF BAGDAD	Conrad Veidt John Justin	June Duprez	Arabia	?	Fairy Tale Arabian Nights D	U.S.	5
ALL THIS AND HEAVEN TOO	Ch. Boyer Jeffrey Lynn	Bette Davis Barbara O'Neill	France U.S.	1846/48	Society D	U.S.	4
SPRING PARADE	Robert Cummings Otto Kruger	Deanna Durbin	Austria	190.	Peasant Girl in Vienna M.C.	U.S.	3
HONEYMOON DE FERRES	Edmund Lowe	Kay Lindsay	U.S.	contemp.	Detect. D	U.S.	2
FOREIGN CORRESPONDENT	Joel Mc Crea Herbert Marshall A. Basserman George Saunders R. Benchley	Laraine Day	England–Holland	Aug./Sept. 1939	Politic, Newspaper D	U.S.	6
ME... GIRL	John Owens	Ruth Terry	U.S.	Contemp.	Dancing M.C.	U.S.	—
MAJOR BARBARA	Rex Harrison Robert Morley Robert Newton Sybil Williams	Wendy Hiller Deborah Kerr Hare Ralph Hare Hitler	England	contemp.	Salvation Army, Religious D.C.	E	8
THE MAN WHO TALKED TOO MUCH	George Brent Rich. Barthelmess	Virginia Bruce Brenda Marshall	U.S.	Contemp.	Lawyer Detect. D	U.C.	3
			U.S.	contemp.	Horse D	U.C.	—
RULES OF THE BLUE GRASS	—	—					
AMOK	Jean Yonnel	Marcelle Chantal	Java	contemp.	Tropic, Sex, D	F	3
SKY DEVILS	Spencer Tracy William Boyd	Ann Dvorak	U.S., France	1917	U.S. Air Force C	U.S.	1

Above Heinz receives a note from the Red Cross

Left One of Heinz's highly critical film grids. See pages 193–7 for his analysis of *The Great Dictator* and *The Thief of Baghdad*

Heinz, Mary, David and Tina in Orpington, 1947

Windlesham, 1981. Left to right: Helene, Heinz, David, Mum, me,
Aunty Fiona, my sister Claire

Then . . . Heinz and David outside 14 Hohlweggasse, September 1978

Now . . . Ezra and me, May 2016

on 7 December 1941. The next day, news reached them of Pearl Harbor.

The conflict had spread by then, with Britain declaring war on Finland, Romania and Hungary because they wouldn't back off Russia. It shows how much things change when he writes about the nations fighting for his adopted country's freedom, the toil exerted by 'the heroic Chinese and Russians'; interchangeable superpowers these days for headlines pointing the finger for some cyber espionage. Heinz says that he finds this period of history inexplicably exciting and it is interesting how involved – at a remove admittedly – he is with the war. Unlike his father, who ignored the conflict once he was out of it, my grandfather is the spectator who goes back to the arena, rather than the bull in the fight who – bruised and battered – does not want anything to do with it any more.

The war appears frequently in his diaries. The attack on Pearl Harbor was clearly an event so significant that nobody scribbling down their thoughts at the time would be able to ignore it; before that there were entries on Greece, Italy, the Albanian frontier. Great detail and snippets, too, from newspapers, fliers and his own sketching hand. A scrapbook of a life.

In 1942, Heinz moves to Chester, 'an awfully pretty English town'. One evening, the family he works for brings up 'the Jewish question'. They are, he says, rather prejudiced against the Jews, which seems like understatement given the Jewish question came up at all. Heinz had to do a lot of explaining, 'to get them to agree that it is all mostly due to jealousy', but the man argued that after the last war Jews in Germany had in fact achieved all the power in finance, business and land. They, he implied, deserved the hate that came their way. A civil interruption from the wife suggests that such influence, if the influence is even true, is no excuse for persecution, but the husband concludes that the Jews cannot understand, or don't like farming.

'I had, of course, an explanation on behalf of the continental Jews, and also pointed at Palestine, but had no excuse for the English Jews,' writes Heinz futilely, and, in all fairness, neither he nor Rudi did enjoy agricultural work, so it is probably best their arguments ended quickly. It would not have been a passionate defence.

The couple concluded that Jews just do not like hard work of any sort. It was surely at times like that, when he thought of the struggle and effort his father alone had been through, not to mention the work he and and his brother were doing, when he does wish he had joined the RAF – for no reason other than the freedom that a cockpit gives its pilot, alone up in the sky and looking down on everyone below. Proving to doubters that he was giving his all for this country. A stubborn assimilation of sorts. I am here and I will belong, no matter what you throw at me.

As the months grind on and Heinz moves from farm-to-farm writing about himself, vaguely, and the war, in detail, and whole paragraphs about what is happening with the weather (27 February 1941: 'An utterly miserable, cold and rainy day' – as if 27 February has ever been anything but), there is no escaping that he was a lonely teenager, half a continent away from his family. This isn't dealt with overtly, often, so when it does come it is all the more powerful.

There is communication between him and his parents, but sporadic, perfunctory – not to mention tampered with and never repeated in the diaries, lost for ever in the cobwebs of some attic in a long-left home. He writes of one letter from Vienna, which arrives with many stamps and postmarks, having been opened by the British authorities and the Oberkommando der Wehrmacht, who stamped three swastikas on it. He doesn't say what the contents were but it clearly lingers like a goodnight kiss.

Maybe it's odd that David doesn't talk about his own, very similar experience, but the lines between him and his son were long and the people guarding them many. So much could have been construed as suspicious and best avoided, so instead all messages from David and Tina to Heinz and Rudi – the ones saved in telegrams – are vague, if loving; they read a little like fortune cookies ('We are strengthened with the firm faith that your path will lead you both to happiness').

They nag, too, from a distance, offering demands disguised as advice. Who to introduce themselves to, the connections they have in London. There is shock, moreover, learned through a letter that Mary sent her family and they passed on, that the party was physically searched at the Dutch border. 'I certainly hope nothing really unpleasant happened to either of you,' reads the telegram. Then it's back to normal: telling the boys that they need to make their beds in the morning, leave things neatly on the wash table, 'and in all other respects take the greatest pains to be cleanly'. In the early weeks, these letters were sent with the frequency some send emails. Mainly about luggage and not spending their money all at once; normal things any parent would tell their children, if they were where they were supposed to be.

David wrote at a difficult time for the family, on 25 December 1939: 'The eighth Chanukah candle is going to be lighted and for the first time we will be left lonely and forsaken with the Torah which was given to us by dear Opapa. We will think about the past times when you my dear children were still here – and your eyes shone brighter and more beautiful for us than all the lights in the world.'

By the autumn of 1941, sometimes Heinz doesn't update his diary for a week, having found occupation and preoccupation, a wedge of settled living that his father took longer to find in his new country. He received a 'sweet letter' from his mother, but doesn't say what was in it. The mentions of his parents, the obvious parallels between him and David, a human wrenching of missing and being missed, are so rare that it must mean something. Deliberate vagueness, perhaps for similar reasons he had for not joining the RAF. He was, it seemed, writing these diaries for nobody, but what if somebody else got hold of them? He was worried about joining the RAF in case the Nazis found out and punished his parents; so if he recorded details, such as names or addresses of telegram marks, were his diaries to be found, they would lead directly to David and Tina. Who knew in the 1940s when or even if the war would end? Or if these farms, mostly in the Royal County of Berkshire, would, in the event of invasion, one day be used by the Germans, despite of course the great superiority of the British who ran them.

Which is not to say a lack of mention means he wasn't thinking about them. On one day Heinz copies out a poem he found in something called *The Children's Newspaper*, called 'A Little Jew in Hitler's World'.

My life is but a nightmare of despairs,
Injustice, murder, suicide and cares;
And like a drifting wreck upon the seas,
I'm left with naught but tragic memories.

Last night I saw my parents shot, and I,
Was spat upon and left to starve and die;
I hopeless, homeless, outcast of the earth;
My only crime, alas, that of my birth.

Heinz nearly died in July 1940. 'Dear God,' he writes, 'there are two things for which I am grateful – that I am still alive, and can write in my diary what I experienced in twenty to thirty terrible seconds. The two things which saved me from a raging bull are my legs and Mr Bryce. After we had finished five hours' work, Mr Bryce and I took a bull to drink, which happens each day. Brock's Hopeful, our first bull, is a wild beast who once broke a worker.' They were cautious. He describes the bull's eyes evocatively as 'swimming, trembling'. Heinz kept him at the water trough at arm's length, tying him to a long bar. The trough was empty, though, so he took him to another. A little later, 'I must, for a moment, have had my back to his face and he – thinking himself alone – sprang forward. I lost the reins over the bar and, in my despairing attempts to reach these, I fell over and – as the bull saw me on the ground – he rushed under the bar toward me with lowered head.' Mr Bryce, who must have been very strong, came to my grandfather's rescue, grabbing the bull and tying him up.

'I am quite unhurt!' he writes, which sounds really English actually, despite the fact he had only been there for a year. 'I am very sorry for all that.' Which, again, is the sort of thing that people who have lived in this country their entire lives say, for things they shouldn't really feel sorry about. He is taking on English personality traits and picking up English phrases. On 18 March 1941, he mentions 'the inevitable everyday trot'.

Seven days later, he visits London and observes war damage he had not seen the last time he was there, a few months earlier. He writes of scarred houses along the Thames, but the 'good old tube' still works. He goes to Tottenham Court Road and back to Bloomsbury House, which he hasn't seen since February 1940. 'It's like a graveyard, dead', the supply of Jews from the continent shut off. His descriptions are ever vivid. 'St Paul's, by some marvel still untouched, stands surrounded by nothing.' Then, in August 1940, he heads one Sunday to Richmond and Kew, possibly the most English of London suburbs. 'Very nice in the garden . . . Played croquet and other games.' If the folder the diary came in wasn't fronted by his swastika-stamped travel documents, you'd be forgiven for thinking you had stumbled across the genteel musings of an Evelyn Waugh character.

He is even uncharacteristically – for a teenager – restrained about women he has feelings for. Maybe he did know that, one day, his father would read his diaries. The Austrian friend Mary, whom he kissed on the ferry, is rarely mentioned after the time they spent at the registration office; the next time a woman is detailed, she is Maud, a Catholic devout enough to be asked whether she would like to be a nun one day: 'No, I'm too modern for that,' she replied. Then, on 2 September 1940, Heinz writes: 'Business and air raids as usual – I am thinking quite a lot about this business with Maud and talking with people about religious matters – surprising what sort of interest an incident like this one can awake! Germans torpedo evacuee ships.' But Maud soon drifts out of his diary and, therefore, for me, his life.

Mostly then, in 1940 and 1941, he tries to be normal, fit in, be quiet and – it seems – appear British. He plays a lot of chess. Has an eighteenth birthday full of presents including *Oliver Twist*. (Some days later he calls the book 'very thrilling'.) Rudi – working on a different farm for a while – sends him a card with a quote from *Rebecca* by Daphne Du Maurier: 'We have both known fear and loneliness and very great distress. I suppose, sooner or later in the life of every one of us, comes a moment of trial – but men and women emerge fairer and stronger after sufferings.'

The day after Heinz's extraordinary diary entry about atoms and humans, and how Hitler taught an entire generation to hate so we shall teach the next one to love, he wrote, 'Again, all day on dungcarting.' On 7 June 1941, he complains of a 'Very miserable day in rainy Reading'. On 24 June he is witness to the death of a man called Jack. 'It is terrible to see a fellow get cheerily on a motorbike in the morning, two minutes later to see him lying in the road, and hear of his death in the evening.'

On 31 October 1940, he writes, 'Italians advance nowhere more than six miles – Half-day, soaking wet, in Reading.' Any employment was on the edge. On Friday, 22 November, he writes that Mr Bryce, who had always apparently held a personal dislike against him and therefore wanted to find something wrong with his work, gave him a fortnight's notice. 'A pity, because I should have preferred to give him notice . . . Though it is a rotten feeling, which I experienced for the first time – to be a sacked man – I'm pretty cheerful, don't resent it and am pretty confident I will find a job soon enough. I'll be alright!' This individual blend of war reports and job hunts continues; the diary of a work-seeking teenager – with the considerable added grief of being stuck in the farms of a foreign country. ('Lousiest paid trade in the country! ; People are going crackers over pedigree stock!') This labour level is where most immigrants start in Britain and I'm fairly sure the above would match the diary of a refugee this century, in the fields around Peterborough, where the documentaries always go.

No, they do not all try to fit in like Heinz did, affecting our phrases and, later, changing their surname. But they are here and they are working when they can

– treated with suspicion and disdain that perhaps encourages them to, later, become a bedrock of society, as my grandfather did, so that people didn't realise he had been anything other than from here, for ever. I guess that he found room for himself on this oh-so-crowded island then; a space exactly the size of himself.

On 4 May 1940, in St Giles' Hall in Reading, Heinz attended an event put on for Young Austrian Refugees. He kept the programme in his diaries.

YOUNG AUSTRIA . . .
. . . is the organisation uniting all the Austrian youth in Great Britain who want their country to be free, independent and democratic.
. . . who want friendship with the English youth.
. . . who want Austrian youth to be taught the spirit of love and loyalty towards their country.
. . . who want to foster the culture and individuality of the Austrian people, and help to make it live in the strange soil of the country which has extended its hospitality.
. . . who feel in a common struggle against the common foe, that they have a bond with the Czech and 'Free German' youth.
. . . who want to help in the building of a democratic Austria which will bring youth a life of freedom, happiness and joy.
AUSTRIA WILL BE FREE AGAIN!

My mum told me that her father didn't talk to her or

her sister too much about his past, but that he always counted in German. A whispered totting up you do just above breath. Something inside he couldn't shake but on the outside, to the world, he wanted to keep in the past. She told me that he barely mentioned his history until the book *The Last Waltz in Vienna*, by George Clare, came out in 1982. He told her and her sister, Fiona, that it was a similar story to his and that they had both changed their names. His from Schapira to Sherwood. My mum and aunt said they had a lot of questions and he said he wishes they had asked him earlier. They hadn't because their mother, Mary, said he still had nightmares of being chased by the Nazis through Vienna. He refused to buy a German car. But, more significantly, he didn't go back to his old city of Vienna to live. His father David did – immediately after the Second World War, back to the place that had forced both his sons to leave and then sent him and his wife off to a concentration camp. It's like being in a holiday home where the roof caves in, breaking the arms and faces of your family, only for you to decide to return the next year. Maybe a local restaurant was just too hard to live without, but still, it feels strange.

Heinz didn't share David's desire to return. There were holidays back to the city and southern, sun-blessed lakes, but no hint at a longer move or – for the rest of his life – any great desire to talk about where he came from either. Instead, Heinz stayed in strange little England, an embittered island he had found full of arrogance and snobbery but where, given a lack of choice and a large degree of affection, he wanted to belong.

That photo in Windlesham was taken in a lovely house with a lovely garden and lovely cat in a lovely village; that could not be more English if it had a football team limp out of a tournament at a knock-out round while the fans beat up locals with chairs.

That is where my family ended up, before moving to other parts of Surrey and of course Vienna oddly, beautifully. (Fiona and her family largely lived in Surrey and then Kent; the Surrey of a Little Bit to the East of Surrey.) Heinz himself made his home in the leafy Croydon suburb of Purley with Marion in a fantastic house offering the finest back garden hill in the Home Counties. These are all very conservative places, safe seats for Tories, where the party can't risk by-election defeats. Very, near-exclusively English save for a few rich foreign diplomats and footballers. I remember once that my mum, in our Woking neighbourhood, went collecting for Amnesty International only to be ranted at about foreigners, immigrants, money and other similar nonsense. How the man's face fell when she told him her father was an immigrant. It is just not what they expect next door in places like Surrey. Nor do they expect immigrants to be white.

Heinz had settled though. Fulfilling at least four of the aims of Young Austria's list above. Feeling welcome enough to stay. Or, rather, more welcome than he would have been back in Austria and so he tries to be more like the people he lives among. In the early years of his diary, he shows a connection to his old country. He does this via his accent, obviously, but also in the ways all of us do, using music and memories to remind us of where we have been. It was hard. The classical music available in Britain in the forties was severely lacking for an enthusiast from Vienna and he writes of being one of a handful of people well-educated enough to maintain a deep interest in classical, or symphonic, music.

From what we know of David, however, music must have kept Heinz close to his parents. It was – apart from simply enjoying the unparalleled beauty and helpful transcendence it offers – one of the key reasons that he actively searched for quality performances in the concert halls of Berkshire. A household filled with music often leads to that passion being passed down and the admiration and knowledge that Heinz gained from his singing and playing father is evident. Beethoven. A brief, but exultant, mention of Handel. Chopin's Piano Concerto in F Minor. The second act of Mozart's *Marriage of Figaro*. This all would have helped him, as music does when it reminds you of home and love.

But music wasn't enough. He soon feels cut off, adrift from his country and other Jews and even though he says he was anything but religious, he misses Rosch ha-Schana, which he would have liked to know about. The more confident that he gets in English as 1939 turns into the new decade and beyond, he simultaneously becomes less like the person that he was when he came over.

His personal life has been more swamped by the political, a home disappearing in his rear-view mirror. It's hard to ignore what would have been happening back in Austria, to old friends and threatened parents and because he doesn't mention them, the panic and fret establishes itself in different ways. Between the lines. In those long sections spent reporting the war rather than the farming stories, as if talking about the war covers up guilt at having escaped it. But the diaries always switch back to England; and to his prolonged attempt to assimilate. He draws maps of farms that he works at. One is called Butler's Lands Farm Buildings and he shows off his new grasp of his second language by labelling Calf, Cowshed, Barns & Machines, Horses, Bull, Pantry and so on. The farm is next to a path called Devil's Highway, used for cattle trucks – taking animals to be slaughtered in sheds. He doesn't mention the specific camps that you know I have in mind, but in a bird's eye view of his pencil squares, and the ramped-up doom in his writing elsewhere, and what we know was happening, looking at the pictures, with hindsight, makes it hard to ignore those camps.

But that is just me, now, knowing what was going on and Heinz was of course ignorant, largely, as most people back then were and he continues in his own world. He had little choice. Work came and went and work was what he needed. He and Rudi spend time after Reading up in Chester, working on two adjacent farms. Heinz pinched apples for Rudi. Rudi pinches carrots for Heinz, who likes to eat them raw. They leave after a few months, in late 1941. Always near a cantankerous line, he is not upset.

'Mrs P proved by her goodbye what a miserable bitch she is.'

The brothers head off to Little Stretton in Shropshire,

where an acquaintance has bought a farm where they will work happily for a while, with a pub, The Green Dragon Inn, as their base. Once there, the distance between Heinz and Austria grew to a distance that would never be cut again.

Chapter 7

I have seen the inside of concentration camps more than my great-grandfather has, despite his being sent to one by the Nazis for two years and seven months. This is a vacuous irrelevance in most ways. He was blind, so it hardly needs saying that as I have watched many documentaries and films about the Holocaust – not to mention museum exhibitions and even visits to the camps themselves – I store visual detail in my memory of the way these places were that he, David, never had.

It is in ways so meaningless as to be embarrassing to type, but it is interesting nevertheless, as it begs some questions of how he experienced the place. By the time he was a camp inmate, he had been blind for a quarter of a century. If he had to rank his senses, as those with a liking for lists do, hearing would have been his favourite as it enabled his ability and passion for music. That, and touch, would have been crucial in a concentration camp for a sightless person. He was able to listen to orders of guards and heed the warnings of fellow inmates. He could feel his way about the cramped living conditions and hold onto his wife's hand as she led him through their ordeal with her eyes working for both, a massive effort to blend into the background and create an existence of minimal fuss. Everything, for pushing on three years, focused on being obedient enough to survive, not so disgusted by what you were able to smell that you retch. Not so fussy with what you can taste that you reject the food given to you. In his memoir, David never really mentions food, either in Vienna where it is wonderful, if you like stodgy plates of meat and oily vegetables, or in any detail in the camp, where prisoners were given a ration of bread every three days to eat with thin, grey soup. I hope it just wasn't of much interest to him. There was no fruit, vegetables or eggs and, despite gas chambers never being built in his camp, tens of thousands died. I know this because I have read about it, and seen the statistics from there. David knew his fellow Jews were dying. I wonder what image he conjured up of their demise, in his strikingly vivid, remarkably positive mind.

David and his wife Tina were deported from Vienna to their concentration camp, Theresienstadt, on the River Elbe, on 9 October 1942. For a while, they had feared being sent to Auschwitz, already known by the Jews who no longer heard from their friends as a place of death. There was also a time when they imagined they wouldn't be deported at all. Special privileges, basically, for the fighting and toil that David had already been through. When the day came and they knew they were going to Czechoslovakia, not that black hole up in Poland, there was a sense of relief, to an extent. My great-grandfather devotes a decent amount of space in his memoir to this period of his life, and I get a sense he thought he and Tina were unlucky to have to leave Vienna at all. He writes that they were on the 'last, so-called VIP, transport'. The 'last' is the word that frustrates him; the VIP bit is telling as to the treatment he had received during the first stretch of the war, which meant he hadn't had to leave Vienna until three years in. And that he did not go to Auschwitz, by that time months into full operation of the Final Solution.

His train held just over a thousand people and it would have taken, at a guess, around seven hours to travel to Theresienstadt. He records nothing of the conversations on board, which is a shame as I can't imagine the journey being silent, but, then again, what would someone talk about on a trip like that? He does, however, explain the demographics of fellow prisoners. 'It mainly consisted of Jews and part-Jews who had been spared from deportation up to that time because of high social position, merit or contributions to the community.' High court judges. State officials. Soldiers. Officers decorated for their services in the First World War. Those severely wounded. It is easy to see why David was low on the list of people made to leave, and in a life full of clouds and very few silver linings, perhaps he was pleased that he was blind. He had high social merit, but then so did a lot of Jews who were sent to Auschwitz. He was a lawyer, but not a high court judge. But take those two merits, and con-sider also that he was also a veteran of a war that he fought for Austria – severely wounded while doing so – and his status among other Jews, to the minds and spreadsheets of the Nazis, significantly increases.

Theresienstadt was a model ghetto, compared to others elsewhere yet, without that piece of shrapnel that flew into his eye and then crept into his other, he would no doubt have been sent to Poland. Tina too. They would, most likely, both be dead. Theoretically, I would still be here, because his son had already escaped, but his memoir would not have been written, with its message of hope. And he would not have been allowed the forty-two further years of life, when he was finally allowed to rest. This is determinist philosophy at its most vivid and twisted. He had to flee East Galicia, but that gave him a city education and a job as a lawyer in Vienna. His pain and depression were severe after injury in Italy and subsequent blindness, but without that he would have been gassed. There is no great working of a god here, as no god is that cruel, but it just goes to show. If you are at your lowest, as Oprah might say, there is always a step up somewhere. He found another forty-two years, happy years, when he was finally allowed to find the best of life.

'When we arrived,' he records, 'there were already about 60,000 Jews in the camp who were living under terrible conditions in old army barracks, in flats and in storage lofts, and who were suffering from hunger as a result of a totally inadequate diet.'

The afflictions and restrictions of Nazi rule began for David and Tina a few years before they arrived in Theresienstadt. They were forced to leave the flat they had written about so warmly in their letters and telegrams to Heinz and Rudi.

It is so lonely and desolate without you. The flat is strange and cold . . . Every object and word reminds us of you and brings such big heartache . . . After your poor, good Papa returned from the train, he fell on your bed, my dear Heinzerl . . . Kissed the mattress and cried, 'My child lay here!' I don't dare to put your things in order . . . That would still hurt too much. I promise you everything that was dear and familiar to you will have a place of honour in our house and be cared for faithfully by me until I am able to hand them over to you again . . . In answer to the question about our lovely flat . . . Nothing has changed in it and it is, as always, the loveliest little spot on earth, because we lived the best and happiest days of our lives in it . . . It was your home in your childhood and youth, and the place about which you think when parents, country and home are mentioned. Everything is still in its old place: school books are in the desk as if you were still going to school – all your library is meticulously ordered and stamps are lovingly kept and stored; as are your small everyday things such as notebooks, pencils, pens, set-squares. Perhaps someday we will be able to bring you all these things, if we should be lucky enough to visit. For the present, however, we feel happiest amongst our own four walls and even though we are also very lonely within them each spot is blessed nevertheless with the memory of your presence.

They had lived there for twenty years, but it was more

than time that mattered. Memories of a life with their children were in every nook and cranny, on every seat and in every sound. I wonder if, when the Nazis made them leave, David and Tina were able to take the presents off the kitchen table, which they had left for the boys.

In the early 1940s, they were moved to a ghetto. Still in Vienna, but hardly a place where they wanted to be. Hitler's initial plans the decade before of a successful and – as the name suggests – fast Blitzkrieg on the eastern front were dashed. It was going to be a longer war and it is around here that the Führer and his commanders decided on the Final Solution, the systematic extermination of European Jews formulated in an agreement dated 20 January 1942. Even before that moment, a thousand people from Vienna alone were sent to Poland in railway wagons, about which David writes, 'Occasional reports which trickled through of the terrible hardships – and fear of death among Viennese Jews interned in Polish ghettos and concentration camps – increased the fear of deportation.' Like Agatha Christie's *And Then There Were None*, but with a sizeable population instead of strangers in a country house.

Members of the Jewish council of Vienna had no other choice, if they didn't want to be deported themselves, than to put together transport lists for the Gestapo. David was lucky, to the obvious extent. He was allowed to advise and represent Jews as a permanent legal representative of the Jewish Association of War Victims. It is bizarre that he was allowed to do so, but the work he did, he writes, was treated, on the whole, well and fairly. If you can accept that anything could be considered well or fair in conditions where a lawyer is necessary to ensure a group of injured soldiers are not taken off to certain death. Still, these invalids weren't spared punishment or humiliation. When the First World War ended, the maimed were given what David calls 'war-injury insignia', a type of medal for those who gave too much and couldn't carry on. But the Nazis banned the Jews from wearing the medal, David concluded.

'One had hoped,' he writes in his memoir, 'that such an insignia would be a measure of protection against rough treatment.'

He hoped other hopes too.

'For my part, I hoped that through my activity as Jewish consultant and as legal representative of the Jewish Association of War Victims – as well as on the basis of my being blinded in war – that I would be spared deportation to Poland.'

This one came true.

Not that his alternative deportation to Czechoslovakia was without its immediate horrors. The conditions were terrible and the death rate, he notes, was high. Malnutrition, typhus, enteritis. They were not allowed to smoke, read newspapers or listen to the radio. But at least it wasn't Auschwitz. In the film *Son of Saul*, set almost entirely in the hub of that Polish death camp, all captive Jews know their fate. They live among ovens and know of their imminent slaughter. But in Theresienstadt, it was different. Of course there were deaths, but the camp had not been built for that specific purpose.

'Although the constant pressure of the Gestapo as well as the severe privations made life virtually unbearable,' writes David, 'most inmates of the camp showed an unbroken will to live.'

Everybody was looking to survive, because with massacres up north, not outside your dormitory room door, it would surely help to be positive and assume there would be an exit someday. David knew that the best way to make it to rescue and another life was to take part in activities that the Nazis would find useful. Farming, cleaning, admin. Anything to help out in the camp or put his mind to use and which, sometimes, came with an extra ration of bread. Some inmates were in Theresienstadt only temporarily and would be moved up to Auschwitz without warning. David writes of the place as if he knew what happened up there, but he is at pains to point out that he didn't. It was all rumour back then.

'We only found out towards the end of the war that hundreds of thousands of Jews, Poles and Gypsies died a horrible death in the gas chambers of Auschwitz.'

But what could he have done had he found out? He and Tina needed to look for ways to survive themselves. Tina worked in the accommodations administration and, later, for a rations dispensary in the camp, while David somewhat unbelievably worked as a 'cultural and entertainment officer'. Not unbelievably due to his talent but that such a job was on offer in a cruel mini-city run by the brainwashed and genocidal. It sounds like the position at a student's union taken by a graduate who is not real for the real world yet. It involved organising talks and musical events featuring intellectuals and artists who were interned. And thankfully for his own sanity, David used his law training too, helping petty thieves from death or further deportation up to the north. In that line of work, he dealt directly with the Gestapo.

A film called *The Führer Gives the Jews a City*, or at least the version I saw, which I found on YouTube, starts off with two men shoeing a cow. Next, some shirtless men smash hammers in a furnace in an industrial rhythm that jars with the music played throughout. That is music hall and bawdy; full of violins. Fairground fun. I pick out Jacques Offenbach's 'Galop Infernal' (Can-Can Music) in the soup, but that is mostly because it features prominently in Baz Luhrmann's *Moulin Rouge*, a film that I have seen more times than makes sense. *The Führer Gives the Jews a City* looks like a government information picture from the 1920s, made to show Londoners what they get up to in the industrial north. Furnaces burn while everybody makes objects. A narrator begins talking in German about how the place was built – the place being Theresienstadt.

It looks like a lot of men working at machines and in front of open and raging fires, but then that is what people did back then. One woman makes a ceramic pot on a wheel. Another chisels a toy horse. It all looks normal and none of them looks upset, but then none of them looks happy either. In fact, they never look directly at the camera. We are shown a quick cut to some warehouses, where people sleep, then back to more work. A printing press. Everyone is so busy and organised. Just before three minutes comes a first Star of David, the type that my family had to pin to their lapels in the city they called home before they weren't allowed to live there any more. Such images remind viewers that the setting of *The Führer Gives the Jews a City* is nowhere near normal. It is a film made by inmates, as instructed by their Nazis guards, between 16 August and 11 September 1944 and, like all propaganda films, from *The First of the Few* to John Travolta's hirsute scientology disaster movie *Battlefield Earth*, it's not very interesting, because you can't believe a frame of it. The film, incidentally, is the same one mentioned in W. G. Sebald's novel *Austerlitz*, when its eponymous character thinks he recognises his mother in the footage. The director was a German Jew called Kurt Gerron, but any control he thought he had was totally illusory, or kept to his subconscious. Once the work was done, he, his wife and all the other principal performers and musicians were taken to Auschwitz to be gassed.

When people died in Theresienstadt, it was down to illness, exhaustion or a rule that had been broken which led to their being shot. Massacres happened elsewhere. In that way, it was an improvement. But, of course, it was nowhere near as free as the film shows. The narrator reads out that work is over and, around the five-minute mark, I think I see a woman smile. The whole performance is ridiculous after all. I can't blame the smirk. From there, the film becomes not unlike an advert for Center Parcs. Workers watch football in an impressive concrete stadium. Arches stretch up three storeys high.

Kids sit on some bleachers. Of course, when the camera pans out it looks less stadium, more prison yard by way of the Colosseum, where the Romans killed their slaves. But the team in dark-grey shirts and white shorts scores just off camera, so some people clap and it looks convincingly fun.

The next scene is in the showers, introduced by a change in the tone of music that stirs deep and ominous strings, as though the filmmaker had heard the rumours, and so toyed with the people the film was sent to, mostly in neutral countries, making them fear for the safety of the stripped and naked Jews. But then the music becomes upbeat. Everybody is jolly, passing soap between themselves. Hanging out. Washing. Then we see the library where people stand and browse or listen to talks. It all seems very civilised, even if the nods and interested eyebrow arches of the audience feel a little forced. On the website for the United States Holocaust Memorial Museum, which holds details for the film, they list notable inmates who have been recognised in this section. They are all from major metropolitan cities (Berlin, Prague, Vienna) and educated sections of society (professor, doctor, judge, historian, daughter of a banker). They are a smart set, who would find all this fakery hard to stomach and harder still to play along with.

Then, just before ten minutes, I think I see David.

I wouldn't trust myself to recognise a man I don't remember meeting, but, well, my great-grandfather wore sunglasses because he was blind, so he stands out, from a sad sea of old men and women listening to a sham speech. I freeze the video. It's hard to be certain. His head doesn't look quite right. I find the photo of him in the garden in Windlesham and hold it next to the screen. It's so tricky. I press play and the man, who may well be David – I still haven't made up my mind – reaches to his chin and gives it a stroke. A universal sign for disbelief and bullshit in the 1980s – and something I will assume was used in the 1940s too. Then, as the camera moves on, he is gone. He is just a statistic at this point, his appearance, if not accidental – nothing is accidental in a propaganda film – then, at least, just that of a man in the milling crowd. Next comes a concert. Unless you're an actor, it is very hard to fake that you are enjoying music, and the audience here cannot help but look completely miserable. Sat at neat, round tables with potted flowers, it's a scene that shows the power music has. That transporting quality as you sit in silence with it swarming around you, and you listen and remember that you are not in a place that you should be. Like when I was in a rare good mood after a sad break-up, but then walked into a bar playing Coldplay's 'Trouble' and felt annoyed again. In the film, it is a room of faces but the minds are elsewhere. Back in their real homes and cities, not the one the Führer fooled the Red Cross into believing he had given to them. The music stops and they applaud as instructed.

Then, I think I see David again.

His dark glasses again stand out. And he's so thin. An enthusiastic clapper, nevertheless. Some generosity for the doomed musicians. And this time it is him. It is definitely him, as the camera shows his profile and I can see what Mum told me when she saw the film, that we have the same shape of head. That is what makes it certain that man is my great-grandfather. A protruding back bit – I don't care what the technical term is – that has been passed on to me. There he is. David. My great-grandfather who had to flee his home in 1914 because he was Jewish, to be moved decades later to a concentration camp, because he was Jewish, to be in a charade of a film while many of his friends were killed and his sons were thousands of miles away, because they are Jewish. And he's applauding. Joining in was the best way to stay alive. That time in the concert, when I was certain it was David, was the first time, other than when I was a baby, I had ever seen him move. And, again, the film carries on, moving outside, where the camp children play in streams while adults plant flowers like it is an allotment of their own, and the idyllic images persist as couples sit on benches and read books in the sun. There is a bit of laughter. Women knit. Children learn. Two pre-teen girls sit on beds holding dolls and rocking back and forth, as though it is a scene from *Life is Beautiful* and everyone's convinced each other that they are on holiday. The version of *The Führer Gives the Jews a City* that I see ends with a glimpse of a family sitting down for dinner, before the film melts away to an end, and I spot a related link to a film called *5 Most Evil Nazi Human Experiments*.

A long time into his life in his new country, spent largely on farms, my grandfather Heinz barely used his diary for over a year. Then on 27 July 1943 he resumed.

A year has passed, almost exactly, since I broke off this diary. It has been a momentous year in my life in every respect; yet I am not sorry that the year only appears in sporadic notes in the diary. For just these events which gave the year its lasting mark, a mark it left on my character indelibly, cannot be put down in writing without distorting their real meaning – and a part-diary is a poor creation, best left altogether. That they, in every detail, will live in memory, is beyond doubt, thus bearing every characteristic of a true record.

He had been busy with work and, maybe, personal affairs which he keeps to himself. Discretion is something the British are supposed to be good at, after all, and he was trying to assimilate. And he's right. His return to the pages is almost a year to the day, with the last complete entry before this one being 22 July 1942. By then he was settled in Little Stretton in Shropshire. But the year of hiatus in his writing entirely corresponds to that first stretch his parents spent in Theresienstadt, more out of reach than before. There are just three pages of bullet points to mark twelve months. Stunning really, if you consider the mind-boggling detail of 1939 to early 1942. So, for example, 14 to 17 August is jotted with extreme meagreness: 'Sheffield (Theatre, Tennis) – from car over the Pennines.' And that is a beautiful car journey. It deserves more. Even worse is the diary for 4 to 31 October: 'Sparkford. Oct 10th: Frome, Oct 17th: Yeovil. Oct 18th: 60-mile bike tour Shepton

Mallet–Wells–Cheddar: two dances.' If the rest of his diary was this short, this book would be a pamphlet, but there are other preoccupations in his life now and it seems, more so than before, that the diary was a comforter to him when there was nothing else. A friend, perhaps, or at least a prop to occupy his time as he shovelled manure around Berkshire. When he returned to writing after that 'momentous year' he detailed how much he had changed his outlook. Once, he had held lofty dreams of employment and achievement, but of 'my own free will', he tore dreams down 'to put into the place of illusion reality – for that illusion would, if carried further, result in tragic and unnecessary disillusion'. He doesn't actually seem particularly bothered by this adjustment. Very zen. He is also a little vague about what the dreams were, yet maybe a year away from the self-involvement of a diary makes somebody less self-involved. But he writes of there being 'comparative ease and little hurt' in his transition towards pragmatism, since 'in our position, reality however harsh must be given first place and dreams be discarded.' Rather like his father in the letter he penned weeks before his death, Heinz stays positive throughout.

Indeed, he says his 'cup was full to overflowing'. Work occupied him almost entirely; 'hard work of body and brain and neither has been beaten'. There was, of course, farming, but new studies to 'open new roads and fresh vistas' were going well and, like a motivational speaker addressing an audience of demolished egos wanting one final shot, he writes, 'The future holds no threat for me. It is for me to conquer it, or vanquish.'

This was all in his comeback entry. A return more glorious than any band's. The bullet points in the year off correspond to his parents' deportation to Theresienstadt, specifically the entry from 4 to 31 October and its information around the 9th and 10th of that month: Frome. But the next scribble is telling in its simplicity. 'November 2nd–5th: depression'. I assume he had heard of their plight by then, even if he is yet to mention it. There is nothing more.

Then, towards the end of his 27 July 1943 entry, Heinz mentions his parents.

> I have met many people of widely different rank and class, intercourse with whom has helped to shape my attitude towards all men and women whom I may encounter. Friends I have added few, but those that I had, have stood the test of time and are amongst my most treasured possessions. Strangely I have only one real boy-friend – Rudi, whose help and calm advice I cannot value too highly. His influence on me and our natural friendship, far above the ties which blood-relation imposes, are beyond assessment. My friends may be few, but one cannot have hosts of real friends. To be popular is good, but to be everyone's favourite, as the proverb rightly says, means to be nobody's friend. Our family is dispersed all over the world, our parents in an enforced exile in a Czech ghetto. Their deliverance, if possible, must be uppermost in our minds.

A programme I watched about Holocaust survivors on an outlier channel of the BBC focused on a man called Freddie. He asked simply, who would carry on telling the stories of the concentration camps when all survivors had gone? His comments were spliced with the usual backdrop of grainy archive shots. Images of the liberation of Auschwitz and Bergen-Belsen rounding up the film's final moments. All prisoners emaciated and stamped like cattle, shot where they lay and ignored by the local Germans, or still alive, just, with grotesque stories to tell. Images like these have become like wallpaper. It doesn't matter if it comes from a documentary or a well-meaning Hollywood film; the notion that most people have of the Holocaust has become abstract, removed from the need for hard feeling, let alone action. There is no sanctimony here. The further we are removed from an event, with more events to talk about in between then and now, the more it becomes natural to leave the past somewhere to be dealt with later, or by someone else, or not at all. It's not like I sit around talking about the Armenian genocide in Turkey between 1915 and 1922. People move on or, effectively, don't care. Holocaust films have become as removed from feeling as emergency room documentaries on television. People die, you feel sad and hope their families are fine and that they didn't suffer too much, but there is nothing else you are able to do.

But Freddie was worried. The Holocaust was, of course, the worst genocide in history. Six million Jews is the number most spoken of and some blame is apportioned to the Germans living near camps, questions of whether they could have done more to stop it. The argument is this: the more aware people are of the past, and the more an entire generation is steeped in shame and misery, the less likely it becomes that it will happen again. When my grandfather Heinz wrote, on 23 January 1940, of building a better world, and having to 'bring man up to a high standard of morale which will make him realise that he is and has to be good' – this is exactly the issue he raised. He wrote that Hitler had 'educated a new German generation to brutality, malevolence, ruthlessness and hatred . . . Why should we not be able to educate the next generation and the following ones step-by-step to this high standard of morale which is to give us the foundation for our new and better world?'

That history repeats itself is of course why the subject is taught in schools, but, all over the world, that really isn't working. The point of history is being questioned. The same week I watched the programme with Freddie I saw a video on the news website Vice which went behind the scenes with Isis and showed similar scenes of atrocity in Syria as I have seen for the whole of my life in camps in Europe. In Germany, the far-right group Pegida is a magnet for the fearful and disenfranchised and attracts thousands to anti-immigration rallies across the country. Its leader resigned when he posted a photo on Facebook of himself in a Hitler haircut and moustache. It probably gained him followers and, while every country has always maintained a far-right element, the difference this century when compared to the end stretch of the last has been its rise in the respected political mainstream. Both German and Austrian citizens, many of whom were alive during the war, all of whom have been taught about the Holocaust, voted for a sort of party or movement that would, at its most extreme, share many of the Nazis' views. Even the smallest fist casts a shadow, but when, as in Austria, the president himself is similar to those that ruled during the country's most disgraceful era, the fist is no longer a one-off punch; a street-brawl when everyone has had too much to drink. It is, instead, a sustained assault and the more fist marks made, the more people are encouraged to join.

The maddening thing is that people find reason for their beliefs in anything. It is not inconceivable that those who are currently leaning towards the ethos of a far-right group would watch *The Führer Gives the Jews a City* and call rumour on the facts of the Holocaust. That was of course its aim. A propaganda film and, like all the puff pictures of its type, if you watch its surface and accept that as all there is, then you will believe what its makers – or the people making its makers make it – want to put across. But my great-grandfather wrote about the film in his memoir and what it shows is that nobody should ever simply accept or believe what they see.

This model camp at Theresienstadt was so bizarre. As the Second World War progressed, the Final Solution became known to the Allies, to an extent. How could it not, with Jews back in the cities where they belonged reporting how their families had shrunk? The Nazis were of course afraid that, if the full force of the horror became known to the United States or Britain, then their war effort would be further stepped up, or bombing raids intensified in that retribution-based manner of conflict. Anything to stop a slaughter already too far gone. As such, Theresienstadt turned into a showroom, polished and photographed to make the best impression. David writes of thousands of his fellow prisoners being shipped to Auschwitz to ease living conditions. As it is hard to make somewhere look relaxed when they keep four to a one-person bunk, the Nazi fix was to kill off the extra bodies. There were, remembers David, shops, a café and a school added. They built the hall in which I spotted him in the film, made for the concerts played by musicians who would later be gassed. There was also a music pavilion. Even a bank. My great-grandfather calls the film a 'Potemkinesque scam'. He explains inmates were told by the Gestapo to look like they are enjoying the café and concert, all that was laid on for them in this theme park that stank of death.

In May 1945, the Russians arrived and liberated the camp. I like to think that David laughed. You know, in that dry way of dealing with the constant shovelling of absurdity that had happened to him since his birth. The Russians. Those who had stormed Rava-Ruska thirty-one years earlier. David writes of jubilation throughout Theresienstadt and a desire and need to return home. Indeed from the way David describes the released prisoners, they feel like a cliché. What had not killed them only made them stronger, mentally at least. Everybody still alive had health concerns they needed to address to make sure they made it through the early days of release.

'Apart from losing a great deal of weight,' writes

David, 'my circulation had become unbalanced as a result of heart damage. One year before liberation, I contracted a typical camp disease: infectious enteritis.' He had not had decent treatment. He had, instead, 'a botched injection', which led to 'inflammation of this nerve which caused immediate muscular paralysis and loss of feeling in several fingers of the right (dominant) hand'. He was treated in Vienna for almost a year, where his usual positivity deserted him somewhat and he writes of a time of depression, as he lost the ability to read Braille.

It never fully recovered.

One thing that strikes me as odd is that David settled in Vienna after the end of the Second World War. He settled back in with neighbours who had kicked and spat at him – who were more than happy to take over businesses the Nazis said Jews were not allowed to run. Memories haunt places. They can be trivial, like a bad fall or a first kiss. For me, respectively, that's a pavement in Austin, Texas where I smashed my arm into a bloody disgrace; and escalators leading to the southbound Victoria Line at Oxford Circus where I kissed my wife-to-be in public for the first time. Memories. Neither place will free themselves of those thoughts and become just places to me ever again, and they are two of the hundreds of thousands of memories that are triggered by geography. It is startling then, I think, that David chose to go back to Vienna. His sons didn't. They stayed in England, but David went back to the country where he would later receive Heinz and Rudi, when they visited with their wives, Mary and Margaret. There are photos of the family by glorious southern Austrian lakes in loose summer clothes, relaxing on deck chairs; to passing eyes just a normal Austrian family on vacation. The sort the country would put in a brochure.

David and Tina made it back to Vienna one month after liberation. Having left Theresienstadt they spent twelve days in Prague, but he doesn't explain why. It was possibly for health checks. Or perhaps the rail infrastructure was damaged so there was no obvious way back. Maybe they really loved Wenceslas Square in the spring. In the Czech capital, the couple 'sent a telegram to our boys informing them of our survival' and, eventually, an 'inadequately covered' lorry took them back to Vienna in cold and wet weather, arriving at midnight on 23 June 1945.

'We were greeted by the sight of bombed-out industrial and residential areas and a deathly silence,' David writes.

They found their friend who had survived the heavy bombardment of the final months of war, to see if they could stay, but their flat had been destroyed. Instead, it was a crowded stay in their friend's mother-in-law's flat for several weeks. Tight and uncomfortable perhaps, but at least there were a few good people who remained. The old apartment that David and Tina shared with Heinz and Rudi for twenty years was still occupied by the state and yet, 'although physically weak and without any sort of public support, we were left to our own devices to get on with building a new existence . . . We had to start all over again, just like when we first started our family as a young couple.' Eventually they gave up on Hohlweggasse, where I visited on my trip to the city, and were given a new flat instead. And David, ever resolute and resourceful, put an advert in the local newspaper, to say that he had returned from the concentration camp and was going to open up his law practice again. He says contact with the 'so-called Aryan population' was smoother than he expected and being in a tumbledown society trying to find its feet again led to an inundation of offers of work. He is very certain why. 'A latent sense of guilt and a certain amount of pity for the few surviving Jewish members of the community,' he says, 'and, not least, a resentment against the Nazi regime for one's own suffering, made possible a restoration of contact between people.' Perhaps such reconciliations helped him write that letter to Heinz weeks before he died in 1984 – this positive notion people can change and forgive being a strong sentiment for a man who had lived through so much death.

Despite [he continues] a great injustice of having to live through the recent unmerciful times – in spite of sacrifices in terms of lives, health, wealth and blood, the surviving Jews had no feelings of revenge and were willing to take up normal relations with the non-Jewish population. The general position of those who survived was that only the Nazis that were most active in perpetrating, directly or indirectly, racist or political crimes, should be tried to the full extent of the law.

His own practice, able to continue, despite his new difficulties with Braille, thanks to Tina's dedication and a lot of hard graft, concentrated on social affairs, using his legal training, free of charge, to help the re-established socialist party while also doing all he could to serve the dilapidated but determined Jewish community. In April 1948, he became the president of said community, another sizeable accolade given swift treatment in his madly busy life, and one that afforded him the 'great honour' of congratulating the first president and head of government of the newly proclaimed Israel – in the name of the people he represented in Vienna – and to accept their words of thanks. Great losses had been suffered. A Jewish population in the Austrian capital that once numbered 180,000, reduced to a few thousand. He writes that 120,000 emigrated while around 55,000 were murdered and drops the line, 'two of my sisters were victims of the planned genocide of the Jews', like it is spilt milk in a kitchen which had burned down long ago.

When David and Tina returned to Vienna, an English officer was able to pass on a long letter from Heinz and Rudi, and from then on, contact was restored. It is funny reading David's sentence take on what his younger son spent hundreds of pages of agonised and annoyed diary writing about, but the early years in England are recorded in his memoir with, plainly, 'During the war they worked hard as farm and forestry labourers in order to get by.'

There is a definite distance between them now. Three months before David's appointment as president of the Jewish community, his beloved Tina died suddenly of a stroke on 15 February 1948. They were married for twenty-eight years, and he calls those years happy. His 'incomparable companion' gone, he writes of his sons as being satisfied in England. They had stayed to belong, when he had returned to Vienna, where they didn't want to return.

'They had their own lives to live,' writes their father of the time immediately after their mother's death, 'and I did not want to burden them in any way.'

That perhaps is the saddest sentence of the lot.

Chapter 8

These days, British teenagers don't really care about the BBC or ITV. In the same way, American teens don't have a clue what NBC, ABC, CBS, ESPN or CNN stand for, the adolescent French don't watch F1, France 2 or France 3, and Korean kids don't know how to find KBS, MBC or SBS on their parents' old television set, the big thing resting static in the lounge, more ornament than entertainment. Everything is in their hands. Phones, tablets, watches, whatever is coming next year – that goes without saying. More importantly, every person they might want to be is in their hands, too. It's not about geography, or their parents, or a certain 'tribe'. It is, instead, in choices they make each day – which depends on social networks, websites, avatars – whatever people from whatever country are chatting about that week. It is easier to assimilate these electronic days – to be a citizen of nowhere. At the beginning of 2016, for the *Sunday Times*, I visited a YouTube Space in Los Angeles; a place for anyone, but mainly the under-thirties, to record what they like to upload internationally. It felt like the future. While there, I met five of YouTube's key posters. Together they looked much like an am-dram group performing *The Avengers*; names and talents were as varied as their appearances. Cenk Uygur was the brashest. His job is to front a current affairs show. He heads, in his words, 'the largest online news network in the world' and either infuriating or bold, depending on your taste, one figure stood out. The average age of CNN viewers is 62–64; for Fox it is 68. His show is mostly under 35. Things are changing, and Cassey Ho – an unflappably optimistic woman who does Pilates – neatly sums up how a YouTube star and the site's users think and hope. 'Moving into the future,' she told me, 'I really believe the world will be one country.'

On Saturday, 5 October 1940, my grandfather Heinz spent a half day in Reading. He writes in his diary that he went to the Odeon to see *Night Train to Munich*. It, as his detail tells me, starred Rex Harrison, Margaret Lockwood and Paul Henreid and told of Hitler marching into various lands and seizing them for the USP of his war: *Lebensraum*. Its story centres on a big factory in Prague and staff there who want to move their scientific adviser – a famous inventor the Nazis want – to England and safety. His daughter was meant to meet him to escort him, but she's arrested by the Gestapo and ends up in a concentration camp. There she befriends a fellow prisoner who tells her of a guard at their camp who has, over the course of the war, turned against the Nazis and would help him escape. Heinz stretches this plot for a further six A4 pages. The scientist father, incidentally, fled without help from his daughter – and has ended up in London. One night – back in the concentration camp – a searchlight breaks and, once repaired, reveals a hole in the outer barbed wire. The couple escaped! They too, eventually, turn up in London, but this is where things get complex. Their escape, it transpires, was organised by the Nazis and now they force the daughter of the scientist to find her fugitive dad, by placing an advert in *The Times*. The daughter is handed a train ticket to take her to meet someone who is supposed to be her friend. I carry on and read more of the plot, but start to skip some as it really is scene-by-scene, and eventually reach a final act on a funicular railway, which seems exciting.

I find *Night Train to Munich* on YouTube. Of course I do, even if I would like to ask whoever put it there why they bothered. Watching it seventy-six years after my grandfather would have been more of a thrill had the film not been so lifeless, so boring. It opens with Hitler banging his fist on a map of Austria and stock footage of Nazis on bikes, taking over parts of the world. That must have jolted Heinz, but soon it comes to the Prague factory where the scientist is working on 'armour-plating' that will revolutionise defensive warfare, where the quick leaps in major plot points become daft. They make plans, show documents, have planes fly over while said documents are being shown, with no time for characterisation. I switch off. It is hammy, with sets that seem to be made out of paper, plummy Brits sat around pretending to be Czech. It is hard, though, for me not to imagine what my grandfather may have been feeling while watching. For instance, it shows that there are Nazis active in England looking for runaway enemies of the regime, which would have been frightening. It also showed letters sent by refugees stopped by those in power and it must have felt like his life was in the movies, even a dull one like this.

My grandfather Heinz loved watching films – and then writing about them. He spent hours-and-hours of free time after he fled to England, more free time than anything else, watching them and as such, they fill up page-upon-page of his diary and surely informed much of his mindset too.

Every now and then, between entries about farming and the war, he maps out a grid on the page and records the movies he has seen. TITLE; STAR (MALE and FEMALE); PLACE (as in where it is set); TIME (when it is set), THEME, COUNTRY OF PRODUCTION (as in who made it); POINTS. The classifications alter a little, but remain fairly standard throughout. *Night Train to Munich* is a five out of ten. (That much plot for a film he didn't even particularly like.) On one of his earliest grids, he has only one star for something called *Skydevils* with Spencer Tracy and William Boyd, which was set in the First World War. I wonder, flapping around for a reason, if maybe it is because that is a conflict he knows all too much about from his father David, with specifics very personal to his family about the destruction it caused – and so has no time for an action film that glibly retells the struggles. But it's impossible to tell. Maybe the film was just rubbish. And from its poster (cheesy; lifeguard on a beach with two giggling women; some planes and a fire) to the tagline

('A Madcap Love Story'), it doesn't look like it deserves much more than Heinz made of it.

But then any link between what he liked and disliked is hard to find; let alone any link between what he saw up on the big screen and what he was experiencing in his life. Posthumously, sat with the diaries, I imagine him writing these reviews: his old country at war with his new one; his parents held prisoners either in a city or a camp, worlds away; him trying to become accepted into a society that, like much of the world, can be hard on newcomers. I think of him like that and wonder how it influenced how he saw the films that he saw. All links, however, are likely to be from my privileged and modern posturing. A post-therapy-era necessity to have all thoughts and actions as deep, or the very least subconscious, when often it is just a thought or an action. (Note my complete failure to watch *Night Train to Munich* without clutching desperately for deeper meaning.)

My grandfather was a teenager in an odd country who enjoyed the sanctuary of cinema and the escapism that its darkness can allow. That could be all; with the added joy that comes when a film is actually good and allows you to forget what it was you were worrying about, so that you can worry about characters on the screen instead. That is much of the point of the cinema and my job is often about pointing readers towards films to lose themselves in. I have never thought that films change society or become a political movement, as audiences are small and, frequently, it is the converted who are preached to, but for individuals? The swamping prowess of a film can not only act as a mind-distracting drug to snap your tedium, but can also put you into a world you didn't know about and – occasionally – want to know more about and, maybe, become part of.

Heinz took this passion of millions to a nerdy level of very few. He was a list-maker, chronicler – with an engineer's blueprint level of detail devoted to the supposed fun of watching films. Someone of that level of obsession watches as much as they can and any political choices will be accidental. He was a farmer, of course, throughout the early years of his life in England, but that time spent watching and rating films – often dispassionately – in very serious grids, means he also spent almost as many of his hours as an amateur film critic; watching the same content as millions around the planet, with nothing changed except, perhaps, the language.

The first film listed that Heinz saw while over in Britain as a refugee was *Let Freedom Ring*, with a tagline from a golden, sadly long-gone era of film promotion – 'Thrill-Blasting Drama of Men and Women at the Turn of a New Era with a Cast as Big as the Majestic Land they Glorify!' It was, according to film site IMDb, released in Britain on 31 July 1939 and such are the further, always startling, depths of the internet that when I search for 'let freedom ring trailer' on YouTube, it is there; with an upload by the account warnerarchive that has amassed a meagre 545 views so far (two likes, no dislikes). The lead in the film is *Nelson Eddy* so, algorithms being what they are, the video chosen to play next in the viewing bar to the screen's right is 'Celine Dion and her twins Nelson & Eddy (2 years old)'. That's totalled 367,834 views, but I never make it to its start. Instead, looped, I sit and watch the trailer for the first film my grandfather saw when he arrived in Britain, just before the Second World War broke out, in some fleapit in London.

It is, of course, in black and white, set on the frontier of the American West in 1868 and, says the warner-archive plot paragraph, has a message of 'religious and ethnic tolerance'. Eddy stands by a piano and sings to a crowd. It's a baritone voice and I guess the whole thing is a musical. 'I'll fight my way and there'll be no whining / I'll find the cloud with a silver lining / I'll find land where the sun is always shining / At the end of the dusty road.' Projection of thought from a reader to writer, decades on, is easy sometimes. Heinz must, I assumed, have found such words profound and resonant. A film star singing straight to him.

I type those lyrics into Google to try and read more. I'm not sure why, but the only source I find with a complete version is sung by a hand puppet lion. A sad 316 views for the lion, but the puppet gives it their all, bellowing the opening lines to the song from *Let Freedom Ring* – called 'Dusty Road' – with real gusto. It goes, 'Got no money / Got no shack / Got to fight for things I lack / So I have got to keep going / Can't turn back / Got to keep bearing this load'.

Heinz must have been in shock sat in the cinema. If he had known about *The Truman Show*, he would have thought this was like that. I flick back to the film's trailer and, towards its end, in what looks like a bar, Eddy stands up above everyone in the room. He sings and patrons raise their glasses and cheer and look on the verge of tears and serious epiphany.

'Where else, but here?' sings Eddy with the power of Adele on the tip of one of her big bridges. 'Are you the master of your own little world?'

On the grid, Heinz writes that the film's theme is 'Freedom' and I don't doubt why. (No, not just the title.) As well as immersion, that is the other aim of cinema: to lend your problems to the story and find comfort by knowing there are other people who suffer like you do. It is also why we read Atul Gawande's bleakly realistic *Being Mortal* when thinking of our parents growing old. The content is sad, but it brings comfort where there will be no joy. A plan, if you like, to cope with something inevitable. I imagine Heinz watching *Let Freedom Ring* in the capital where I now live, knowing that he is not alone; how others have fought in the past like he must now, have been forced to flee their homeland but that eventually he'll be OK. A master of his own little world in this new country.

He gives the film a zero, less than I'd give *The Phantom Menace*.

He's a tough critic, then. *Bulldog Drummond* – the second film he watches, with a theme of 'Deceit' – is also awarded nil, while John Wayne's seven-time Oscar-nominated *Stagecoach* – the American Film Institute's ninth best Western of all time – was given only two out of ten. His favourite film from his first half-year over in England was *Pygmalion* – George Bernard Shaw's play that would later become the musical *My Fair Lady*. The tagline for *Pygmalion* was, 'He picked up a girl from the gutter and changed her to a glamorous society butterfly!' While I would like to pontificate about the conditions Heinz had fled in Austria and the class-obsessed country he was trying to fit into, and whether that is why he loved the rags-to-riches story of easily-reachable society and gave him, a farm boy around Reading, hopes of becoming more, it's too risky after how much he hated *Let Freedom Ring*. Maybe he really liked *Pygmalion* as he was a big fan of Leslie Howard as Professor Henry Higgins and mostly went to the cinema because he loved the snacks.

Often, his diary entries are a dovetail between farming, war and cinema. On 30 March 1941, Heinz writes of two destroyers and three cruisers from Italy that were in a naval battle three days earlier. The next day, he is off to see *The Thief of Baghdad* and only mentions the war in a most fleeting way. 'An extremely nice evening at the pictures where I saw the colourful film, *The Thief of Baghdad*, an Arabian Nights story. A beautiful fairy-tale, which I liked all the more as I am getting fed up with present-day-event's propaganda-pictures.'

It's hard to avoid how different his cinema-going was to that of the people he had left back in Austria. Not his parents but his peers. A page of his diary includes a cutting from a newspaper under the headline 'Shows Wrecked', which detailed something that happened in Vienna. In a cinema in the second district, a type of bomb, 'a cross between a firework squib and a light bomb – stink-bombs, secret newspapers and leaflets, brush and paint', had been thrown into a screening of a Nazi propaganda film called *Baptism of Fire*. It was being shown to the Hitler Youth but some of those who remained, Jewish and non-Jewish, were brave enough to begin a fightback, in a country that often didn't seem to want to lose its occupiers.

'Sneezing and itching powders were put into ventilation flues, to blow in with "fresh" air!' reads the British newspaper report with much unhidden glee. 'Effective in scattering a Nazi audience.'

Back to *The Thief of Baghdad*, and its five-and-a-half pages of plot. I have no idea why he writes out so much plot. Maybe he was practising his English. Perhaps farms for people who don't like farms are very boring. 'Once upon a time there was a Sultan in Baghdad, Ahmad was his name (John Justin, good) – he was hated and feared by his people, as under his rule terror and prosecution stole all freedom from the people. But this was not Ahmad's fault, but an evil Grand Vizier Jaffar's (Conrad Veidt, brilliant) fault, who was behind all the daily executions and scourges.' If you'd like to know more, the DVD is available on most major online shopping sites. I don't need to watch it, though, because I read the entire way through this plot, via a scene 'where in a terrific castle in the statue of some deity is a crystal in which one can see anything one wishes to see'; another where 'Ahmad is taken to Baghdad – but his attempt to save the prisoner is unsuccessful and – captured – they both are sentenced to die the next morning'; all the way to a final sentence where the flying carpet is mentioned and the future great hope, Abu, is 'off, off to find adventure'.

Next day, 1 April, he mentions that, 'an impressive list of important people who escaped the Nazis was given yesterday', and it is back to the black and white of reality. There are very few exceptions where he allows the facts to mess with his fiction. He goes to a cinema. He thinks about war. He goes to a cinema. He thinks about war. But then, similar pages of over-the-top plot are given to Charlie Chaplin's *The Great Dictator* and, for once, it is easy to discern the political from his affection for a movie. It is an anomaly. The Chaplin, he says, is 'the greatest satire, and most biting parody on dictatorship, in particular the one of Hitler, combined with the most stirring story of Jewish sorrows'. He writes of the audience 'roaring with laughter' at the mimicked Hitler speeches; he notes the accuracy of the depiction of ghetto life with its 'brutal storm-troopers who patrol, plundering all streets', which he knew about from Vienna. There is more of his obsessive plot and I am impressed entirely by Heinz's memory, even describing with comic – if perhaps unintentional – understatement that 'it is impossible to describe everything that happens; everything a farce, biting parody on Germany'. But of course, in this rarest of films for my grandfather, some sentences other than baffling levels of detail creep in. There is a speech to a group of soldiers in which they are told, 'Fight for liberty, democracy and human brotherhood!'; the diaries record the audience reaction in a Reading cinema as being 'moved, as it only could be after magnificent words spoken by the little man Charlie Chaplin to every man and woman in the world'.

He goes on: 'It should be printed in millions of copies, distributed all over the world – also dropped over Nazi-occupied Europe. Its effects must be great.

What, I think, is the main feature of the film, is that Charlie does not depict the dictator, but the maniac, the ridiculous, dangerous fool, Hitler. For me the greatest, most unforgettable event for a long time – maybe a lifetime.'

So he liked it. Almost as much as I enjoyed *Donnie Darko* in 2001, peering up, leaning in my seat next to my friend Matt, eyes popping at the innovation and brave new ideas the likes of which we had never ever seen. I didn't have anything deeper to draw from, like my grandfather did. No war. No great loss. My parents less than a mile away, at home. It affected me because it was a personal story about a boy and his mother and a girl he loved. Heinz had bigger things going on. So moved is he, that he wants to see Chaplin's *The Great Dictator* again and again. 'If I had paid ten pounds,' he explains, 'I should not have regretted it for a minute.' Given that £10, in 1941, is worth £352.95 in today's money, there is little doubting his enthusiasm; and no doubting at all the main reason he latched onto the film in the first place.

I watch it for free, on YouTube of course; a place that copyright lawyers seem to have absolutely no control over. The film begins with a scrawl: 'This is a story of a period between two World Wars – an interim in which Insanity cut loose, Liberty took a nosedive, and Humanity was kicked around somewhat.' And as Trump takes office and undoes much of the decent work his predecessor did, while my own country faces years of economic uncertainty, I think about printing that opening out and pinning it on my wall, to what end I do not know. *The Great Dictator* still looks great; expensive, expansive, everything *Night Train to Munich* wasn't in terms of cinema. I think of *Dr. Strangelove*, obviously, and the humour has lasted well. Chaplin was a genius simply because he fulfilled the definition of that word like very few do and, when he dances with an inflatable globe in his dictator's palace, grace combines with satire to create a weightier, weirder punch.

The final, sombre speech is worth repeating in full.

We have developed speed, but we have shut ourselves in. Machinery that gives abundance has left us in want. Our knowledge has made us cynical. Our cleverness, hard and unkind. We think too much and feel too little. More than machinery we need humanity. More than cleverness we need kindness and gentleness. Without these qualities, life will be violent and all will be lost.

It is sad that I can watch a film, decades after my grandfather, and nod along at the political points being made. Sad, yes, but also I like it, a little. We share this piece of art; two men leading very different lives, but feeling the same thing, and it makes me think we would have had so much in common, if we'd had more time together.

But yes, that film is a rarity. And there was no great move to seek out political works after that, in case they match *The Great Dictator*'s wonder and power. It is so hard, then, to escape the key reasons that seemed to take Heinz so often to the cinema. Escapism. Worlds to explore. A sense of being normal and sharing something with people over the world. Being like them. Being not like himself. On 12 May 1941 – five months on from his Chaplin revelation – he went to see *Major Barbara*, which was based on another play by George Bernard Shaw. He seems to have really liked his work. The dialogue, he writes, was 'witty and bitingly ironical'. But that's only the beginning of the review. The acting, he gushes, was 'the most brilliant I ever saw'. He then lists the cast and concludes it is impossible to say who was best. The plot is tangentially about war, but it is not the specific war happening at the time and, besides, the themes covered, explains Heinz, are more social justice and poverty. 'The whole thing is to prove that poverty does not make happy and, also, that a fellow who produces weapons of war is not necessarily bad, and can make others happy even with his blood-and-sweat produced millions.'

It was 'most delightful, the best picture ever', he enthuses, which shows real political maturity and understanding of a system that had so shaken up him and his family. I've no idea, but sort of dread how much he'd have been willing to pay to see that one again. He had to eat.

Film after film after film. On 11 June 1941, he goes to nearby Wokingham for a change, to a very good Odeon. There, he watches *The Man Who Talked Too Much*, which was a 'rather good and original detective film of a lawyer-criminal with human mind', followed by a film so bad it doesn't even warrant the inclusion of its title, only a slamming four-word 'rubbish about racing-horses'. Five days later, he heads back to the cinema in Reading and waits patiently in a queue for an hour to see a film by the name of *Amok*. Made in 1934, it had been banned by censors for years – hence the queue – probably because it has a plot brimming with intoxication and infidelity. Heinz was 'thoroughly bored'. *Love on the Dole*, 24 August 1941, had themes of socialism that criticised the system. He gives *Robin Hood* five out of ten; *Gulliver's Travels* only two. A movie called *Freedom Radio* with the theme 'Anti-Nazi' gets half-marks. He also goes on dates. Or, at least, to the cinema with a woman. *One Night in Lisbon* on 22 October 1941 was with Madeleine Carroll. 'Very beautiful,' he writes, but no more detail is given. I know more about *Night Train to Munich* than I do about her.

On 7 July 1941, just before leaving Reading for work up in Chester, Heinz writes, 'And now for my farewell visit to the pictures at Reading, where I had spent so many pleasant hours during fourteen months. I saw *No Time For Comedy* – an extremely entertaining, witty comedy with Rosalind Russell, James Stewart . . . Assisting: *Gaucho Serenade*; western sing-song, cowboy stuff, not too bad.'

He sounds so normal when writing about film; a man on Facebook, just back from the cinema, who wants to share his thoughts with his followers. He is not Austrian or Jewish or a refugee or English, or stuck in the middle in fear of not making it across a border, or missing his parents, or afraid of deportation, or being in a job he hates, thinking of joining the RAF, or worrying about his brother, or putting up with people not liking him and his brother, or receiving army-stamped letters from relatives in Vienna, or finding out the latest happenings in concentration camps.

He is, instead, free. As free as everyone in the cinema, watching something made thousands of miles away, but which plays for audiences all over the globe, without change. Heinz was enjoying films in 1941 when the world was at war and far more spread out than it is now. After reading what he thought of a variety of films, I don't think of him as someone looking for political interpretations, but instead somebody looking for anything but the political. He wanted to forget the nationalism that had got him to where he was and instead revel in something more accepting and universal.

His final grid of films, from his diary at the time he was working on the farm in Chester, shows he was still as harsh a critic as you can get. Very few poster quotes from his reviews. Only a point for *Lone Wolf* and *The Witness Vanishes*. Two apiece for a double bill of *Train Robbery* and *Gay City* (a film that the internet has no mention of sadly, but makes for an interesting Google search). Apart from *Love on the Dole*, which has seven out of ten, they are all given five or less. All genres, or, as he calls them, Themes, are capable of displeasing him. Cowboy, War, RAF, Song, Wild West, School, Flying.

There is no country he prefers either. England, USA, Poland, Cuba, Portugal. They all, according to my grandfather, were making very average movies. At least, though, he was seeing them; each viewing making him less just the teenager from Vienna that he was when he came over, more the individual he made himself become later on, settled in Croydon with a British family, a safe distance away from the country in which he was born and where most people who were born remained. 'Where else, but here? Are you the master of your own little world?' would work as a catch-all for all that was happening to him in England, if only he'd liked the film it was from.

When I lived in Vienna, there were three cinemas that showed films in English, and I went every month. *Jurassic Park* is the one I remember most, but others, perhaps oddly, stick out too. I have no idea why I remember *Accidental Hero* starring Dustin Hoffman so vividly. But these visits to the cinema were sanctuary for me in a strange city of people not speaking my language and fellow students who called Marathon bars Snickers. I was watching and experiencing everything old friends would have been back in Britain at the Odeon at the top of the high street in Guildford, the only difference being adverts before the film played in German, not English. But with the international environment at my school, I was pulling away from them too; creating an individual who was part-British, part-Austrian, mostly the world. Upon my return, these films – *Jurassic Park*, really – were what I was able to talk about to people who had stayed in Surrey. Films and football. Such was the glue to blend me back in a bit and make me a little less of an exception, in those bright-green jeans and weird baseball top, and, twenty years on, such shared topics would have increased. Each country maintains its own culture to an extent, but teenagers, whether in

New York or a refugee on an eastern European border, have access to, and enjoy, the same videos, shows, music more than ever before. The systems that spread stuff across the globe are becoming increasingly available to people. So, not only would I have stayed in touch with all my British friends, but when I went back to Britain, I would have stayed in touch with friends from Vienna, too. I was really good friends with a boy from Indonesia. We talked about everything, nothing, shared enough interests. I know nothing of Indonesia now.

'Moving into the future,' said optimistic Cassey Ho. 'I really believe the world will be one country.' Thing is, I wanted to believe her so much that, for a few weeks, I ignored that statement's naivety. If access to everything the internet has given her, plus those who share her view, had been around in 1994, I wondered if I would have been upset at leaving Britain in the first place, or sad to leave Vienna on our return, because it wouldn't matter which country I lived in. As long as it was safe. A breakthrough in sociological combining, owed to shared communication and cultural consumption. Facebook friends from all over the world. Getting Likes from my Sikh mate. All YouTube that we all watch. My favourite programmes on Netflix. Constant messaging on Snapchat or whatever service has replaced it by the time you read this. The world now moves with a pace that means it is harder or indeed pointless to put down roots. You can feel at home anywhere.

In a way, that's what Heinz was trying to achieve with cinema when he was a new refugee in Britain. Cinema always feels new because what you are watching is new

CHAPTER 8

and, back then, that was a way – indeed, the only way
– for him to feel that he was part of something positive
being created in the world. In doing so, he started to
believe he was fitting in somewhere.

I consider the internationalism and newness of the
internet as a cinema max of sorts, full of exciting ideas
and a world becoming one. I hoped, once, that it would
usher in a new era of understanding. A 'Declaration of
the Independence of Cyberspace', written in 1996 by
one-time LSD-devoted counterculturist and Grateful
Dead lyricist, turned expansive thinker, John Perry
Barlow, links with such optimism.

> Governments of the Industrial World – you weary
> giants of flesh and steel – I come from Cyberspace,
> the new home of Mind. On behalf of the future, I ask
> you of the past to leave us alone. You are not wel-
> come among us. You have no sovereignty where we
> gather . . .
>   . . . We are creating a world that all may enter
> – without privilege or prejudice accorded by race,
> economic power, military force, or station of birth.
>   We are creating a world where anyone, anywhere
> may express his or her beliefs, no matter how sin-
> gular, without fear of being coerced into silence or
> conformity.

Maybe this has happened, among the generations below
me, the under-30s; those that have always had the web
and know how to use it. But more and more it rather
feels like we had a chance, but are going to blow it.

It takes less than a minute of searching around many subjects on the internet to feel as if you would rather punch yourself in your own face than speak to anybody again. Ho and her people almost had it right. There will be fewer countries moving into the future. But it doesn't look like being one.

Rather, it looks like two – each one retreating further and further into their own pockets of will, making it harder for dissenting voices in deep to be heard, as they're coerced into the conformity Perry Barlow was venting against.

Assimilation is what Heinz wanted when he came over to England and, after some initial distrust and confusion, he made such a settled and integrated home for himself that people he met for the first time didn't know about his past. Maybe it will be harder to do that now. Not only does everyone have their history set in coding – my grandfather's status updates as a refugee coming up on Facebook's memory feeds until the day he quits Facebook. But, also, the voices that would be against him settling here have found new platforms they can shout from and more people than they had before to back them up in their opinions.

Heinz had the cinema when he was a refugee. It made him feel normal and like others who were sitting in the dark with him. If he was a refugee today and wanted to be online, he'd probably never leave the house, and not because he was enjoying it. I remember my coffee and cigarette with Adham Alrumhain back in Vienna. That Syrian made entirely of nerves. On various farms, with various locals, Heinz had his detractors, but he never experienced open and volatile fear to the extent Adham had and was showing in that café. From his diaries Heinz seemed to enjoy his new country, not look over his shoulder to see if anyone was clenching their fists behind him.

I interviewed a pop band for the *Sunday Times* a few weeks after the EU referendum. We had cups of tea and talked about politics. The duo were both sixteen and did not understand why people voted to leave the EU because of worries about immigration, since they were at school with lots of EU migrants and many of them were their friends. Not a threat to employment but, instead, the same. A level playing field. Inclusivity. Cooperation. That was what the young women were talking about and how naive I became when I left, think-ing – it was quite soon after Cassey Ho's enthusiasm in California – about the internet, and schools full of the result of decades of border movement, meaning children growing up side-by-side, like I did in Vienna, meaning people won't think of passports and borders when they are older, but, rather, just think of a human being, and that they are all equal. I found some hope. But, I was speaking to a pop band – a profession never threatened by freedom of movement of workers, or the number of asylum seekers let in. When a prime minister talks about British jobs for British people, it's never because there is a possibility a couple of Romanians are going to take over Blur's rhythm section. And post-referendum, as news came in of hate crimes, teenagers attacking foreigners in the streets, bottling Poles outside a kebab shop, it struck me that, due to the internet, their echo chambers had already formed. And, because everything is programmed to make you stay in your chambers, algorithms pushing stories to your feed that they think you will want to read, I find it hard to imagine those two women in a band ever thinking differently about immigration, in the same way I can't envisage teenage boys who beat up eastern Europeans sitting down for a meal with friends from Warsaw at any point other than in prison.

In this way, the world has got worse and it's hard not to conclude that it is up to individuals to make their part of it as nice as can be. That sounds like giving up but options are few and most days, I leave the world alone and concentrate on my own home. When we lived in Vienna, I remember various efforts that led my sister and me towards thinking that our past wasn't as simple as it might seem. My parents were behind this because they wanted us to know about these things as such knowledge would help us become the people they want us to be. Looking outward; not staying insular and yelling.

We all went on a family cinema trip to see *Schindler's List*. Heinz's second wife, Marion, used to send videos to us from England. Some bought, others were things she had recorded off the television and while, every fortnight, that included a recent episode or two of *Casualty*, it would invariably have some documentary on the Holocaust, too. Titles like *Children with a Star*. We had a four-CD set of music from Theresienstadt; a string ensemble nobody thought was the greatest audio recording of all time but kept listening to anyway. Then

one weekend while living in Vienna we all drove to
Theresienstadt. Sadly I can't remember any of the trip.
My parents went to Auschwitz, too, but I wasn't allowed in as there used to be an age limit of thirteen and
I was twelve, so my sister had to stay back in the hotel
in Krakow with me. We watched MTV all day and ate
Mars Bars. A David Bowie song, 'Jump They Say', was
on hourly rotation. Perhaps staying put had as big an
influence on me as going, but either way, effort was
being made. We were being tethered to our wild past.

I wound up here because of all the things they did,
and what all parents do to their children, plus the
other sparks we come across in our lives, and I will
push this history onto Ezra and hope he becomes an
outward-looking citizen. But it is sad that I feel defeated, that I feel like shutting myself away from the world
because, really, what use is speaking out about anything
since all you do is back up an opinion of someone who
agrees with you, or push somebody who doesn't to scar-
ier extremes. Maybe I don't belong anywhere but from
my own home, with my family. I know that takes me
back to the beginning of this book, and why I didn't use
to think of my past much, let alone the Syrians trying
to have a future, because I was self-sufficient and lazy.
But when I read my great-grandfather's memoir with a
passage about positivity in future generations, then my
grandfather's atom example, of how the next decades
can be good; or my parents teaching about a history
that tore my family to bits, only to see history repeating
itself – then it becomes too hard, if I am honest, to
continue believing the world can be a better place. It's

tempting, isn't it, to buy up some locks and use the convenience of the internet to bring what is needed to us. Everything out there will upset us. What if we all stayed inside? Where else, but there, are you the master of your own little world?

One page in my grandfather's diaries is titled, 'Books I Have Read'. He liked lists. I think he would have loved the categorisation available on iTunes for all his classical favourites and I wish I could have shown him how to use it. The titles that I instantly recognise are *A Short History of the World* by H. G. Wells – who lived in the town that I grew up in, Woking – and *Gone With the Wind* by Margaret Mitchell, a book I have never read of a film I struggled to get through the one time I tried. Other authors on the list that I know are Erich Maria Remarque, Émile Zola and Charles Dickens, while there are topics, too – Beethoven, Mozart, The BBC From Inside which show both Heinz's interests and a preoccupation in discovering what this country that had provided an alternative, better future for him was really like.

If those books are the holiday reads, the rest though tell the story. That of a man clearly very bothered. *The Jewish Problem* by L. Golding; *The Internment of Aliens* by F. Lafitte; *Germany Puts the Clock Back* by Edgar Mowrer. This is where he was being serious. Cinema, it seems, with its flippancy, variety and international pull, was something else for him. First, of course, it is a communal experience. You can listen to what people think as they leave the room. Nothing was as serious in a cinema as when he read, alone, and who knows where his copies of the three titles above are. Lost in a farm in Berkshire, no doubt. Or left on one of his trains. But all have mentions on the internet. Not a great presence, admittedly, but enough mentions in various places to reveal what they were about.

The Jewish Problem, by Louis Golding, was published in 1938. Golding was a Manchester-born Jew of Ukrainian descent, mostly a novelist who is forgotten now but he was popular at the time. He wrote non-fiction, too, and the title of this book does much of the work of a synopsis; especially when you know the author was Jewish himself so is hardly likely to be anti-Semitic, which its title could suggest. Over on Goodreads, a user called Apoorva gives it five stars and writes, 'the title referred to the problem the Jews have faced down the ages, rather than to a suggestion that the Jews were a problem! In fact, at one point, the author suggests an alternate title for the book – The Gentile Problem.' This sounds wry, and given the couple in Chester who said one night to Heinz and his brother, Rudi, that Jews do not like hard work, it is easy to imagine my grandfather reading this and laughing to himself, maybe flicking a V-sign behind closed doors to his employers in a different room. I know I would. The user on Goodreads continues, writing that Golding's book is a concise history of how and why the Jews have been persecuted through time, their stereotypes and myths. The final point sticks. 'As I glanced through a chapter on The Nazi Horror,' writes Apoorva, 'I realised that while there's a long list of various atrocities, there's absolutely no mention of the Holocaust. I thought that very strange! I then checked the publication date. November 1938! I am still in shock. What would this book read like if it was written six years later!?!'

There is more on the internet about the next book on the list, *The Internment of Aliens* by François Lafitte, published in 1940. I find a blurb for a reprint from 1990 and it is clear why Heinz was reading it. 'This book,' goes the blurb, 'was the first to focus public attention on the mass . . . indiscriminate internment of German-speaking refugees and political exiles in Britain.' My grandfather was scared.

Finally there is *Germany Puts the Clock Back* by Edgar Mowrer, published in 1933. Mowrer was an American journalist who was based in Berlin; a brave reporter of the war that was starting and the organisation behind it. In 2012 his book was included in the *Wall Street Journal*'s Five Best list of Reporting on 1930s Germany and Hitler's Rise. The book begins with a description of Weimar Germany, and the freedoms within it. 'It is hard,' he wrote, 'to conceive a much more tolerant society.' The parallels with the rise of the far-right in today's politics after an age of liberalism barely need to be typed. The stale and afraid always react to a glittering aura of freedom for all. In the *Wall Street Journal*, it says Mowrer foresaw Hitler's success and Germany's march to disaster long before most of the world. He describes the Nazi leader as 'the most effective orator in Germany and hardest working politician in Europe', at a time when, apparently, too many were dismissing him as a clown. The author noted in his memoir years later that he warned Jews to 'Get out, and fast.' It isn't a surprise Heinz read this. He probably read it twice, and it is hard to think of a more choking example than these three books in the whole of the diaries. They were being read in the early 1940s by my refugee grandfather and libraries should stock them today.

Chapter 9

An email arrived from another Syrian refugee waiting on his future in Austria, on the day after I had met up with Adham Alrumhain in that traditional Viennese café where we split his packet of cigarettes and he insisted on paying for our coffees. I didn't have time for this second one because my wife and I had made holiday plans. Movement entirely up to us. I did not want to explain this to a refugee: 'Sorry, I can't meet you today, but I have an ecolodge hotel booked in rural Slovenia that I need to get to.' I made up an excuse instead and asked him questions over email to try and make him feel like he hadn't wasted his time – and to make me feel better about myself too. He replied within a few hours; another person trapped in this endless movement of put-upon people twisting round the world. I have no idea where he ended up.

I am from Syria.

I am 30.

I come to Austria in 14.02.2014 – and it was very difficult to arrive to hier. I was in Turkey and I was going to Greece, Macedonia, Serbia, Hungary and after that I arrived to Austria. The journey took two months.

I come to hier alone, all my family in Syria.

I choose Vienna because I was thinking I will find my chance hier, because I am geology and I want complete my master in Vienna university.

I like Vienna and I wanna stay hier forever because I have political problems in Syria and my city in Syria (Deer Al Zour) is destroyed.

I wanna stay hier and work hier. The people in Vienna is friendly but I cannot say 100% because many people have scary from refugees.

I was learning German fast as you can't live here without German language. You can't study in university or you can't work. But now I can speak good German and I have accepted from Vienna university for master and I work for my certificate in Zentralanstalt für Meteorologie und Geodynamik in Vienna.

I have also many friends from Vienna and they help with language. I feel safe here, but really I have scary about future because I don't have nationality. My Syrian passport was finished and I have here just travel documents.

With travel documents not every country take my visa and I think that not good.

I did not find hier racial discrimination against ethnic, but people here hate all foreigners do who not integrate quickly into Austrian society.

I wanna answer all your questions. Really I am sad as we are don't meet, but maybe in another time. We are friends now and nice to meet you!

Best regards,
Mahmoud Hawas

There is a bridge in Walthamstow, four minutes' walk from where I live, and the gaps in its brick are filled with a corrugated iron fence, and a mess of brambles and leaves. The gaps are big enough to spot trains through, running below every fifteen minutes – two at a time, one on each track, from and to Liverpool Street. It is where my son Ezra likes to spend his time. We have bought him toys. A plastic bus that makes noises. A set of musical instruments to bang and shake. His nan found him a wooden kitchen in which he cooks a fake pizza and offers it around to guests. But all the toys and energy in the world won't take him away from that bridge. 'Choo, there,' he says, pointing from the kitchen in the general direction of the trains.

Since having a toddler is about caving in so you can have an easy life, my wife and I fold and, rain or shine, walk those four minutes to the bridge, to stand like weirdoes and wait for an eight-carriage commuter train to rumble on past. Sometimes, the driver will wave. Every time, Ezra gets excited. The mad and simple de-light in his face is so infectious that for a while I had failed to think of the bigger picture, to the neatness of the bridge on that route. But now I do. Those tracks lead to Liverpool Street, where Heinz first alighted in Britain. As I often state, to the level of pub bore, *without him arriving, I would not be here and Ezra would not be here.* When I think of this connection, of the circle closing up, all of me fills up with satisfaction. My son stands cheering a train on the route that his great-grandfather took. My son has a Jewish name in his memory and the memory of family before Heinz, in East Galicia, which once was Poland, but is now Ukraine. All the previous connections that struggled and survived and so made him exist.

That makes me happy, but there is guilt too; born of the inaction and negativity I mentioned when I was confronted with a reading list in the diary my grandfather left. That ceaseless cycle of pain and human disappointment, plus a real sense that my generation had failed, and lost their opportunity of being part of a wider and kinder world, offered to us – perhaps – via the internet. This led me to think that we might as well just give in, concentrate on our own families and problems, not thinking of the next Heinz who needs a country.

That was, I think, where I left you.

Stella Creasy, my local MP, has an office up the road from me in a cute villagey bit of Walthamstow. She is the type of politician who provokes opinions because she actually engages with her electorate, finding time to address both the bombing of Syria and the possible retraction of a car-free scheme in her constituency, the so-called Mini Holland. She is also outspoken about the need for Britain to take in more asylum seekers and refugees and, as an MP in an area of high immigration, this isn't a careerist move.

I meet her at her headquarters – the only building on the road that hasn't had a gentrified facelift – possibly, the only one in the village that doesn't sell feta-stuffed olives. The part of the country she looks after is the part of the country I have found to belong. She is exactly the sort of politician who would have welcomed my grandfather to this country and has in the past talked about Kindertransport, and whether something similar could be done for the children of Syria. I keep my own inaction quiet, as we sit around an eighties-classroom table.

Dressed in an old Stone Roses T-shirt, she is far from the stereotype of the British politician. We have tea and I spot posters for the London mayor Sadiq Khan on the wall. At that point I had a Labour Muslim mayor; female Conservative prime minister, Theresa May; female Labour MP, Stella – two of whom campaigned vehemently to remain in the EU and another who possibly did but ever since seems so delighted the country voted to leave that it is hard to remember her saying anything that didn't serve her career. It's been tough, of course, since that vote, for anyone foreign living in Britain, and Stella tells me of an Italian grandmother who is nearly eighty sobbing down the phone asking if she will be sent back to Italy. All the woman's children are here. All her grandchildren too. I once thought, the old lady says, that this is where I belonged.

'Everybody is uncertain,' Stella says. 'It is so destroying for people's social fabric to suddenly feel uncertain about your place.' How big an issue, I ask, is immigration and refugees? 'It's massive and it's come to define, for people living here and now, what the world looks like – in the sense of whether you are defined by your thoughts and feelings about the issue itself or your thoughts and feelings about what other people think about it. Britain is a very divided country right now. Wherever you go, it is a topic – and I don't think this was the case ten years ago – that people feel they have to have a view on.'

It is, she continues, being used as a cipher for concerns about other issues, as life in general became harder for loads of people around the world. It has become separated from discussion about community cohesion or the economy, and what effect it may have on them; it has, instead, just become an excuse. A red herring. I mention a hippie hope to her. That of the unflappable Californian Casey Ho and the impressively bearded LSD champion John Perry Barlow: the idea the world could, online, become more at one with itself and free of the borders that cause so much division.

She listens patiently, as politicians need to do. Sipping tea and no doubt dreading the vast sacks of post at the front door, nine-tenths of which, I imagine, don't contain an impressively stencilled compliment and flower-press spelling out her name. She is often on Twitter and Facebook, so is significantly further advanced with the internet than most of her colleagues, but this experience has not pushed her towards some utopian ideal of what we can achieve online. Rather, technology is one of the symptoms of a recent chasm in societies around the world that liberals thought they had closed long ago. Austria. France. America . . . Britain; globally, either a split among populations half to the left, the other half far to the right; or a general shift of the right to the further right.

'People sense that change is happening very quickly,'

she says. 'That the world is moving very fast and, so, what is their place in it? And that is not an unfair concern. Lots of generations have dealt with big issues. Poverty, civil rights. But they've happened very slowly. If you think about social and economic change in the world, not just in Britain, the pace has become so quick, people are seeing it before their eyes. That is disconcerting, because things you took for granted are moving very quickly, whether technology, social mores or cultural change. That's very unsettling.'

She says that she has jumpers that are older than the internet. Nieces and nephews, she explains, swipe at televisions and more like all is an iPad, as 'they just expect the world to move around them'. She was forty when we spoke and that's the age of people who had to adjust to the internet, not use it before they can walk. Many, therefore, have struggled to make it work for them.

'The difference I would draw,' she explains, so quickly and coherently it makes me realise how mid-witted many actors that I interview are, 'is between people who feel they have a sense of control about the world ahead of them and people who don't and so feel very excluded and, perhaps, antagonised by others they think do have control. The idea there are some people for whom this new, crazy fast-paced world is working for, and there are some people for whom it's not. And whose fault is that?'

This briefly reminded me of the line in Perry Barlow's utopian cyberspace doctrine: 'You are terrified of your own children – since they are natives in a world you'll always be immigrants. Since you fear them you entrust bureaucracies with parental responsibilities you are too cowardly to confront yourselves.' How simple it would be just to wait around for the elderly to die off and make everything OK. That is, after all, what a lot of younger voters said after the EU referendum. But when Stella mentions ninety-year-olds who love living in a diverse part of London, then fifteen-year-olds saying 'pretty hairy things about people from minority communities who they will know because that is the world they live in, but their sense is that they cannot control what is going to happen to their future and therefore you've got to find somebody to be cross with . . .' Well, when she mentions those examples, Perry Barlow's trip ends as dramatically as a jack-knifed multi-truck pile-up in a tight tunnel.

The subject of echo chambers comes up. 'We've never been more connected and yet more isolated,' says Stella. Is society actually worse, I ask, thanks to everyone being able to find support for anything they want online, however dangerous thoughts may be? She says neither yes nor no. Thinking of David and Heinz and their endless source of goodwill, I ask if she is optimistic. 'Wherever you live in this country,' she says, 'we want you to be part of building its future and if you're not, that is a problem for all of us, because we miss out on what you're capable of . . . So what is it we can give you that lets you go out and take the world on rather than be fearful of it?' That is her message. 'I would not say I'm optimistic,' she decides. 'I'd say I want to do my bloody job.'

Stella's parting thought is this. 'When I hear, "There's too many people here." Or fears about Muslims . . . The initial reaction is, "Aargh, that's terrible or uninformed." But actually, no . . . You have to put aside your own preconceptions to go, "How can I help you change that to something that gives you a better option?" Because if I thought it would be better for Walthamstow if we built a wall around the whole of Britain I'd be the first digging. What is better for Walthamstow is a Britain that's open, confident, tolerant. But we haven't won that argument with people.'

'It isn't a bad life on the whole!' wrote my grandfather Heinz, in a diary entry from 1943. 'Only let the war be over soon! Then life will begin anew . . .' He was in Shropshire at this point, in a time when, in his still new life in Britain, he sounds most relaxed and at home. It isn't even relief any more. Rather, it's settling; like a frisbee, thrown, still wobbling, just about to land.

On 17 April 1942 he started mentioning a woman called Pamela. 'I have found a friend,' he wrote. There had been a visit to the farm, from a woman and her daughter, Pamela. 'We sat together on Sunday evening for a chat that lasted till half-past-eleven and took a spontaneous and immediate liking for each other.' She was twenty-two – 'unaffected, pretty, natural and irresistibly likeable'; a student of medicine. He was younger, but had lived more life. 'How extraordinary our understanding was,' he wrote, 'I was to find out for certain after only three days.' The pair had been taking walks, talking until midnight, each day and then one walk, one Wednesday, he says he'll never forget.

'The things she told me then,' he explains. 'The way in which she confided in me, a perfect stranger after all, was so extraordinary that I could not but feel that I had found a girl who was miles above any I ever knew.' She told Heinz that she was engaged to a colleague, but that her affection for this man was 'deceptive' and therefore she planned to end the engagement. Heinz was the first to know, and she was telling him since their understanding had been so immediate. My grandfather didn't find this odd. 'If any other girl but her spoke to me like that, it would have made me – to say the least – a bit funny, but it all came out with such sincerity and candidness I could only feel proud and happy about having found such a friend.'

He writes that he misses her when she has to leave to head back to Sheffield and that he fills his time 'going to the pictures so often that I really don't remember what I've seen'. There are visits to places like Rhyl. Distracting excursions. Seeing what is to be seen. Then, on 6 May, he writes between updates on the weather and the war that, 'Meantime, I am writing to and getting letters of incredible length from Pamela.' On 22 July, he announces that he's off to Sheffield for a few days, having had five telephone calls with her in four days. Next comes the diary's break, the bullet-pointed sections that skip months. But her name still appears in June the following year, 1943, before disappearing (like so many relationships we have in our twenties), into a shoebox in the attic, the photos never to be looked at again.

This, to me, is the most normal thing. A young man dating a woman and breaking up with her or her breaking up with him. (I am only guessing that they dated.) It was another removal, for Heinz, of the idea he was restricted to one culture, that he was always destined to be that Jewish refugee from Austria in a country he will be a stranger in for ever. When one native treats you as an equal, like Pamela did, there is no reason why others can't follow suit. He was, to her, just a man in England. How wonderful that must have felt to him.

He has friends as well. At a party, he writes proudly of being chosen to be Master of Drinks, where he sat on the floor surrounded by a 'baker's dozen of bottles of various drinks which I mixed in the most atrocious manner . . . We laughed a great deal – and had a good time in the sweltering night which had followed a scorching day.' In that passage alone, he started with a medieval English phrase, before using two choice British words for hot. He heads with Rudi back to Reading, to visit some old friends, and says they felt immediately at home. Everything in the diary by now appears so strikingly normal and British it reads like a forties take on Adrian Mole. Annoyed at being back from holiday, Heinz at least has an easy day because his boss is off. Later, he retires to his room to listen to a Dvořák symphony, and then tries to avoid a colleague he can't stand.

On Sunday, 8 August 1943, though, he reminisces.

What a day for an anniversary of such tremendous importance. Four years ago: that was the thought which flashed across my mind several times, during these last few days. What came after, its graveness and consequence, cause for so much thought and philosophising, did not preoccupy me much. Only the strangeness of parallels . . . Whilst I sat in my bath on Friday night, four years ago we were for the last time in Grinzing [area of Vienna], eating – before going to see, for the last time, the twinkling lights of Vienna in the Danube. Yesterday morning while we had our break at ten, four years ago our hearts were filled with indescribable anguish and sorrow as we said goodbye at Westbahnhof . . . Last night at seven, as lights went up at the pictures, four years ago, Nuremberg. Today at ten in the morning as I got up, four years ago I stood with one leg in the concentration camp during those anxious minutes at the Dutch frontier. Now in the evening, just as we are going to play bridge, four years ago, we disembarked at Harwich, set foot on English soil for the first time. It is all very strange.

But that is all and, then, it is back to that normal life of his, continuing in its unfussy, low-key way. He talks of days off work allowed for rest, which he admits really mean laziness. Then he writes of hobbies that are unimaginable, had he stayed in an Austria still being battered by the war and essentially free of Jews. Such as, 'yesterday we had a fine two hours of tennis'. There is still very little mention of David or Tina, but when Italy surrenders on 8 September 1943 the entry says it is the 'greatest day of the war'. He turns twenty and he says, jokingly, that he is old. But that is fair. Only people of my privilege can feel young at that age – given that the only adventure and confusion lies ahead of us, when we have to fend for ourselves.

Then, all of sudden, he starts to mention friends and contacts in Croydon – where he would end up and my mum would live before going to university in Bristol, where she met my dad and the two of them started finding places for our family to live in beginning with the letter 'W' (Windlesham, Woking, Wien, Weybridge, Walton-on-Thames). A man called Kurt Weisselberg, whose sister had secured the papers that allowed the Schapira boys over in the first place, offered Heinz and Rudi a job, if they could secure the release from their farming work. Over whisky, they talked and my grandfather is thrilled. It was a non-farming position. He asks for a release from his farm on 1 October 1943 for which he gets a nod – 'Great day!' – and this agreement is made official five days later. His spirits are thrillingly high, and he even allows a little sentimentality to creep in. He says he has grown to like that countryside around Shrewsbury, and even found time for the people he dislikes.

'But then,' he reasons, snapping himself away from schmaltz, 'there's no reason for undue sentimentality, for I hope to improve my position considerably. Kurt has found me temporary digs, so I shall travel on Tuesday. The farewell at the mill was dull . . . Italy declared war on Germany – a travesty, a farce, sickening!'

And here is where the diaries end.

He is home.

Weisselberg was a fellow foreigner, a German, who, like Heinz, would change his name to something anglicised: Whitby. He was the founder of wood firm Parker Timber, where my grandfather worked for the rest of his life. When he died in 1985, a trade mag offered the following.

'Heinz Sherwood – an appreciation . . . In 1943, he joined Parker Timber where he become managing director in 1973 and, subsequently, the chairman. He was chairman of the National Softwood Importers' Section of the Timber Trade Federation in 1972–73 and then spent four years . . . first as vice-president and later as president of the Timber Trade Federation . . .'

More accolades follow, before it ends: 'Mr Sherwood's death is a great loss to the timber trade, and he will be missed by all who knew him.' The homage mentions his 'native Austria' at the start, but after that it is all about his accomplishments in the business and the nation. Austria feels like a different story, one that ended a long time ago.

I feel remiss in not mentioning my other grandparents, but both my grandmothers, Mary and Laura, died before I was born. I have seen pictures of them, but would not be able to pick them out of a wedding shot. I wish that I had more to say about both. Albert, my grandfather on my father's side, lived just past 80. I remember him well enough and I do so fondly. The man who kept Fruit Pastilles in a cabinet in his kitchen, and whom we drove to see every other weekend in his flat in Horsham. He died when I was thirteen in late summer 1994, the summer we arrived back in England from Vienna. The last four years of his life, therefore, barely factored into my own, save photos of when he came to visit us and we went to Prague, he and I at a tram stop, me in a fluorescent tracksuit, of course. The years before, however, that decade or so of my life before moving abroad, it was Sundays watching *The Chronicles of Narnia* on BBC sat cross-legged on his lounge floor, my parents doing the catching up and my sister and I looking at that magical snowy world on TV. How strange it must be to have to leave your home during a war . . . It is odd, stuff you remember and, even more than Narnia, my most vivid memory of Grandad was the day that my dad tried to demonstrate a cheese slicer to him, but ended up cutting his own thumb instead, Red Leicester blotted with blood. Albert was eighty the year I turned ten, and we shared a party with an uncle, John, celebrating his fiftieth. Such is my other main memory but that's pretty much it. I was too young when he died, Fruit Pastilles and BBC TV, the sweet age, and there is no memoir through which to catch up with him later on. Regardless, him, and the grandmothers I never knew: they all have as much to do with me as Heinz and, indeed, David, but I suppose – unlike those two – as far as I know, they were never threatened enough to flee, or had to face prejudice about religion or nationality. In a way, despite getting only a paragraph in this book, they are, therefore, members of my family who are the most like me.

I have been wondering about the emphasis of the title of this book. Where, if I was an extravagant newsreader,

I would hammer down on a word. I don't think it is the 'I' as, often, as with both my great-grandfather and my grandfather, people travel looking for a home for their family. They travel in certain groups and so do I. Wherever I belong, Ezra and Rosamund must belong too. The 'I' is, really, a 'We'. The emphasis, too, should not be placed on the 'Must', for that implies a certainty, some sort of given and of course an alternative exists. Wherever you go to that you think you might belong in, there's a good chance you will be sent back. And I wouldn't pick out the 'Somewhere' either. It's simply too vague. Most people have a destination in mind when they flee or emigrate. There is no somewhere, rather, 'there'. So, I think, the answer to the question of emphasis in the title is 'Belong'. I must *belong* somewhere. And I *belong* in London, somewhere that welcomes my mix made up of some Jews and a branch of distant Huguenots on my mum's side, a Britishness on my dad's, so far as I know. That isn't even that exotic; most of the other people who live near where I do, and belong here, are further mixed up from places far wider flung. If our society is such a wild soup of ingredients, it strikes me that we may as well make it taste better for everyone, rather than looking to stick our hands in it, to try to pick out some tomato that long ago lost its shape and became part of a wider flavour.

It is interesting how quickly my grandfather assimilated. Marion – his second wife, and the closest I have ever had to a grandmother, a devoted and wise woman whom you would always want near in a crisis – wrote a book on Tennyson called *Tennyson and the Fabrication of Englishness*. In the dedication, she wrote, 'To my late husband, Heinz, who came to England at the age of sixteen as a refugee from Nazism and had to create a new – English – identity.' They married in 1976. When over coffee in the British Library, where she still goes to carry on her research into the poet, I asked what this dedication meant, she told me that her husband had become 'more English than the English'.

Indeed, she says she had more Jewish friends than he did when they met. He had married my grandmother, Mary, in 1946 and joined a local tennis club in Croydon in leafy south London, a place so close to Surrey it is essentially in Surrey. Marion says his diaries ended when they did, in 1943, as he was busy and satisfied. He had stability and a job that wasn't on a farm. He really did not like farming. For Parker Timber, Heinz worked in the offices, initially selling wood, and then rising up the company. A respected job. An English wife. A tennis club. He was doing all he could to fit in and it reminds me of Adham, the way he insisted on paying in that Viennese café and Mahmoud, who emailed me later, saying that Austrians hate foreigners who don't integrate quickly. All three men wanted to fit in. Heinz was no doubt helped in that aim by the fact that he was white. Marion adds, with some bewilderment, that when certain neighbours came to his funeral, they were surprised to learn that he was born in Austria and had lived the first sixteen years of his life there. His surname was Sherwood, yes, but very few English people are called Heinz. It is remarkable what people don't care about when they don't think about it.

She says he had become so British in his manner-isms and customs that he once took his hat off at a Jewish funeral on a return visit to Vienna and offended the guests. He hated going back to Vienna and would say that, despite their shared experience as refugees, he and his father had nothing in common, due to the length of their separation. There is a parallel perhaps in David settling in Vienna after the Second World War, but revisiting Rava-Ruska only once, and his son who stayed in England and only returned to Austria out of duty. If the place you were born in kicks you out, you resent it and become, instead, drawn to the place which provided a refuge when you first needed it. But, mostly, as Marion and I talked about her husband and my grandfather, she smiles and says, a little sadly too, that he never really talked to her about his past. It is what my mum said too. His past was distressing, of course. But also, there is a sense of the stiff upper lip; and there is nothing more British than that.

After three months in this country, my grandfather was using very British phrases. After less than a year, he was playing croquet. It took him no time at all to start moaning about the weather. Do people saying that we have too many immigrants really believe none of them will ever contribute to society, or fit in, if that's what they want? Logically, that must be their position. Immigration, they think, not only fails to add anything positive to the country but, also, immi-grants stay labelled as such. They wear a badge of not belonging.

That position is terrifically forgetful. As hypocritical

CHAPTER 9

as Leave voters cheering on a foreign national in their football team. Or waving Union Jacks during the Olympic summer, drunk on national pride only to, four years later, vote in the hope that the eastern Europeans who had come to east London to build the arenas where our athletes triumphed would be forced to leave. But Heinz's origins were misapprehended even during his lifetime. And, after a generation, it can become impossible to tell who is originally from Walsall or Warsaw.

So, I ask Stella, do people forget this? Not only the buildings and infrastructure that needed plane loads of foreign hands to construct, but also that most of us have family history in a foreign country, not so far back? Do a rising number of anti-immigration Brits forget they are immigrants too? 'I don't think they forget,' she says, considerately. 'It is that it's suddenly becoming contested as to whether that is part of our identity, because debates about British identity are coming to the fore.'

When Theresa May made her first party conference speech as prime minister, she said that if you are a citizen of the world, you are a citizen of nowhere. It is worth nothing that, in Germany in 1933, someone said, 'It is a small, rootless, international clique that is turning the people against each other – that does not want them to have peace. It is people who are at home both nowhere and everywhere – who do not have anywhere a soil on which they have grown up.' That was Adolf Hitler.

I put May's speech to Stella. 'A citizen of the world,

231

for me, is about compassion,' she says. 'And my worry is she's trading off patriotism against compassion. Compassion and tolerance always used to be a very proud British value, and she's stripping that out.' This goes back to what Cameron said even before his British values speech on the day of the centenary commemoration of the First World War. That article in a newspaper about the Union flag, football and fish and chips; those 'British' things.

'These are anchors,' says Stella. 'And what Theresa May is doing, as far as I'm concerned, is saying to people, "Yep. The world is moving really quickly. It's frightening and we should go back to some mythical time." Which didn't work for everybody . . . The 1950s and '60s were just as elitist, if not more so than modern Britain . . .

'Because what I think people are proud of and patriotic about, is when Britain has been leading the way in innovation – whether that was in the Enlightenment or Victorian era. There was a real sense we were creative, dynamic and went out into the world and shaped it and were at the heart of things moving. You wanted to come to Britain as that is where things were happening.' She's worried that Britain might be reverting to a stale sort of insularity, a backwater, the type of country, a bit like Switzerland, where a general consensus is let's hope everyone doesn't notice us.

But rather than getting all adolescent about it, and slamming the door to your own home – let alone your country – she is determined to change the world back to the way it had been most of my life, a way of life many liberals thought was set in stone. One whose borders mean less and where internationalism is the popular route forward. She is focusing on interaction, trying to build relationships. People dismiss it as a bit fluffy, she knows that. But she wants to get people involved. A collective action in an embedded multinational society is surely a far kinder place to raise children than the only other option which is an enforcement agency driving their vans about to kick out foreigners at dawn.

'The future for me is about networks,' she explains. 'I want everybody to interact. In some ways, it's a more active vision than integration, as integration implies everybody becomes the same. Actually, for me, it's about everybody treating each other the same . . . I say you've got to behave in a way where you can talk to each other as equals.'

We shake hands goodbye and I effectively sign up to join the local party, go along to meetings and help her to try and change the world. With passion and drive that could energise a stoner on their third day in Amsterdam, her emphasis on the need for humility is sorely lacking on pretty much every side. Figureheads like Donald Trump aren't the issue here. When they have gone, their supporters remain, and we need to work out how to make them not vote for someone like that again, rather than laughing at them on a Twitter feed they will never read. Stella isn't suggesting that immigrants go to the extent my grandfather did in changing their names, and having everyone believe they have been British their whole life. She just wants us all to accept the modern world as it is, and start to make it work for everyone.

This is because – back to that soup again – all ingredients have been chopped and chucked about. A few still stick out the same as when put in, but others are fully mixed in – so it is impractical to change now. Rather than boiling it up to a temperature so hot that it spoils, let's take it off the heat and serve it up just right to enjoy. A spoon for all. A flavour for everybody; and, if successful, I promise never to use this metaphor again.

Back in Vienna, after surviving years in a concentration camp and having to endure the too-soon death of his wife, Tina, my great-grandfather started helping the Jewish community settle back into the Austrian capital, to be neighbours to Gentiles who turfed them out by welcoming the Nazis into the country. In his memoir, David briefly mentions his sons and what happened to them after the war. There is a distance between them now.

During the last year of the war, they found opportunities for advancement within the timber industry. They also had good contacts with English families and married English girls. However, we were not able to be present at the weddings, since there still was no way to get to England from Austria. This was especially hard for my wife as her hopes during the years of separation, to find and care again for her 'boys', were severely disappointed . . . It was only in the summer of 1947 that we were able to visit our boys in England.

Seeing them called up the strongest feelings in us, after
so many years of privation and worry.

After that, though, he writes mostly about his own life,
back in the city that must have held the strangest of
memories.

By February 1948, David was alone. He had not
wanted to 'burden' his sons so, instead, he worked.
Indeed, he says, he overworked, stating that keeping
himself busy 'helped me to at least deal somewhat with
the terrible turn of events and my loneliness'. His sons
visited annually and he says the key to being a widower
is an ordered lifestyle and close friends, not to mention
some respect from the community too; the holding of
a position that makes himself essential to others. This
was how he was for six years, until he married his
second wife, Helene, who was in that photo in the
garden in Windlesham and whom I met many times
when we lived in Vienna – barely able to communicate
since her English was limited and my German terrible,
but finding enough smiles and gestures to get along
quite memorably.

'Thanks to her intelligence,' writes David of Helene,
'and her understanding of my situation and her loving
character my life took a normal and generally content-
ed course.' After the war, as he worked and worked,
he became more and more successful as a lawyer. It
was only on 31 December 1970 that he gave it up. He
had suffered from a hearing problem in addition to his
blindness, and the combination was too much. Also,
in fairness, he was seventy-three. Largely, though, over

and above his profession, he drew the most satisfaction from that key role that he held in rebuilding the Jewish community – making them belong somewhere again.

He sounds content on the last pages of his memoir that come under the header of Final Comments. Settled back in the city he had fallen for as a boy from Rava-Ruska, he writes that he dreaded retirement. He had been out of work for five years by the time that he put his life story together and, looking back, says he could not imagine satisfied living, without a regular occupation.

The physically and mentally normal retiree, especially one whose vision is intact, has many possibilities to occupy himself in meaningful and relaxing activities and in this way be able to fill in the excess of free time, even if he doesn't pursue a regular hobby . . . Walks in a city chock-full of sights and stimulating activities, theatre, cinema, exhibitions, as well as trips to the nearer environs and most of all extended journeys, absorb much of this time and add to one's knowledge . . . The sight-handicapped are totally excluded from all of this.

He says it is only in retirement that the blind really start to know that they are blind and subsequently suffer. But there eventually emerges a studious zen to him now about blindness. He writes that it's a scientific fact that sight counts for 80 per cent of sense impressions; that therefore it is the 'most serious of this sort of handicap and the hardest fate imaginable', yet, somehow, he turns that into a positive of a sort, saying, 'this unfortunate condition can to a great extent be mastered and turned to an advantage if one possesses the will and ability to resign oneself in the positive meaning of the term, that is, to let go of that which cannot be brought back – but without giving up hope, and use possibilities for education, rehabilitation and reintegration in society which are widely available.' He means special schools and institutes, libraries packed with Braille books and audio recordings that offer knowledge in pretty much any field you would want. He also counts himself as fortunate, as people blinded at any earlier age than him would lack his spatial awareness. He knows colours, forms, the sights of nature and has 'a realistic notion of the world' around him.

'Life will,' he concludes, 'on the whole, go fairly smoothly . . . What would be more important for the blind person would be acceptance and not exclusion as an outsider . . . The traditional prejudice, as well as the doubts and inhibitions in dealings with the blind, should also be put aside. For this, only good will is needed – something surely of which everyone should be capable.'

It is probably rude to take the words of someone who is no longer around to stop you, and turn them into a meaning you know they didn't originally intend, but that paragraph about coping with blindness in a judgemental world is far too good for me not to pinch, and apply its sense to what Stella means when she talks about inter-action and what Heinz found in England thanks to his great striving and some kindness from others; indeed, what David was trying to make happen for him and his fellow Jews back in their blighted Vienna. Everybody helping each other out, no matter where they are from. It is easy for people who consider themselves the norm and majority to reject difference, as interacting with difference takes work. It is also easy for the majority, in times of difficulty, to lash out and pick on the different since they are ones who are not like them. David, a blind Jewish refugee and victim of the far-right, had been put upon his entire life. He had more reason than most to shut himself away, but not only could he find the forgiveness to settle back on the same streets, but also write with such beauty about how to live your life when significant obstacles have been placed in your way. It isn't just the memoir and how it ends, but that letter to Heinz too, and a hope despite everything that man isn't as awful as his experiences may have led him to believe.

'For this, only good will is needed, something surely of which everyone should be capable . . .' There are some lines from an old Charles Bukowski poem that make a mad comparison only suitable in part for this book.

'There's a bluebird in my heart that / wants to get out / but I pour whiskey on him and inhale / cigarette smoke / and the whores and the bartenders / and the grocery clerks / never know that / he's / in there.'

I must reiterate. It is only suitable in part, but perhaps that bluebird is the positivity that David so often writes about. This is just Heinz's atoms argument in a dead poet's voice, but a bluebird must be in everyone. And such a message and story is needed now. Marion wonders what Heinz would think of a diary he wrote as a teenager being brought to the public. I wonder if he would feel a little embarrassed but she decides that her late husband would probably feel very proud.

Chapter 10

At the back of one of the two folders that hold my grandfather's diaries is a family tree. There are question marks the further back it goes, but it is up to date; Ezra is there, alongside his cousins Chloe and Amy – my sister's two daughters. Right up top is Wolf Holin, who married Rebekka. They had six children, but only four of their names are known – Michael, Isaak, Rose and Paul. Isaak married twice. First to Amalia and then to Fanny. Isaak and Amalia gave birth to David, my great-grandfather, and two others; while Isaak and Fanny brought five children into the world, one called Simon. We know all about David. He married Tina and one of his sons is my grandfather Heinz, who ended up in Britain. Simon – whose surname was Holin – married Gina and fled Vienna to reach London in 1938, just before Kristallnacht, and then, later, travelled further to San Francisco. Their son is Elliot. These days, he is a rabbi in Pennsylvania at a congregation called Kol Ami – Voice of my People – in the Elkins Park suburb of Philadelphia. His family is, pretty obviously, very religious; unlike Heinz or his family. The two men are equivalents on the family tree, both allowed to be as they wanted – in the United States and Britain, respectively. I emailed a link on the Kol Ami website, and so did my mum, but we've had no response from our distant relative. Oh well, I don't answer half of my emails either and, besides, I know enough about him from what I've found on the internet. We are very different people, but traceable back to the same place, barely one hundred years ago, the results of a violent world which was open enough when our ancestors needed it to be, but is closing up again now.

In the middle of nowhere in Ukraine, quite frankly the most remote and vulnerable I have ever felt, I spent hours looking at a train track but never saw a train. The roads were bumpy and the towns appeared by stealth – so empty and small they have often gone by the time you realise they were towns at all. A train service – no matter how infrequent it is – feels essential in a place as bare as this but, as I'm driven around by a young, angry man while my mum, dad and translator Olha are engaged in almost endless historical chat, I stare out at this track which we cross numerous times, and wonder where the trains are. We drive all day. Lunch a packet of crisps and a bottle of water from a service station. But even when standing in the garage forecourt, I could spot the tracks and so know there was no train. Again and again, through town after town, no visible means of decent public transport to help people move about or leave.

Seventy years after the end of the Second World War, a memorial was erected in the west Ukrainian town of

Rava-Ruska. It's made up of gravestones, two sloping walls that rise to a point which doesn't quite meet in the middle; a gap that allows its visitors to look at what's out back – long grass and wood edges, where more victims are buried. The memorial, you see, is on the spot where Jews jumped off transports that were taking them to death camps. The whole area around Rava-Ruska used to be very Jewish. Black hats and long beards: such were the common sights, say the few old enough to remember. Jews accounted for half the 12,000-strong population in the 1930s, but the memorial marks a mass grave where at least 3,000 lie buried. The other thousands were killed elsewhere and a plaque near a scattering of burnt-out tea lights is inscribed, in Ukrainian, English and Hebrew: 'Between 1941 and 1944, Jewish life in Rava-Ruska and the surrounding area was eradicated by the German occupiers.' On top of a rusty pole by the gravestone wall, a metal Star of David sits like an afterthought. A pile of smashed tombs clutter the yellow lawn. This is work in progress. A memorial to a dreadful past, put together by a few organisations who cared deeply about the removal of life in the town and so funded a movement to tell new generations what happened and what to avoid.

After half its people were murdered, Rava-Ruska re-built itself and now has a population of 11,000. It looks calm as I am driven in – very agricultural French in fact. The locals mill around – distracted, vaguely content. The town square is busy with couples pushing buggies and new building work. It is a town that looks at first glance as though it has a future, but then compared to what I had seen on the outskirts of nearby Lviv, any open space would appear somewhat hopeful. Back there we drove past block-upon-block of tumbledown flats, fractured window panes with tarpaulins for glass, walls like wet cardboard and, on every corner, people loitering only because they didn't want to be inside. In Rava-Ruska however, my first impression was that locals seemed to be outside since they had somewhere they wanted to go – even if they had nothing to take them there very fast. Three petrol stations line the first hundred metres of town, but most of the routes out are barely suitable for vehicles.

The Jewish memorial is down a road pot-holed like a ski mogul course. On the way to it, the main roads – refreshed for football's European Championships in 2012 – had been largely smooth. Especially the ones that led to Poland, the tournament's co-host. There had been barely any erratic swerves by the young driver, Oleg, a man who's so furious at his government he would often take both hands off the steering wheel, just as a bus pulled out and his dashboard flashed up a warning that read like a eulogy. That was on the good routes, ones we drove on as he talked about government corruption, and explained that the roads in Ukraine are bad as the people in charge of them spend all the money for asphalt and maintenance on their own homes. It felt like histrionics, and I assumed that the tarmac was to Ukrainians what the weather is to Brits. Something to complain about when, really, it's not that bad. Then, I got it. My legs juddered up and my neck jarred as Oleg turned off Rava-Ruska high street to the road leading to the Jewish memorial. The car wobbled, only able to reach a speed of 7mph, and bounced – surfing hard jelly as I tried to sip my bottle of water.

As Oleg parked, I watched a wiry old man on a battered bike struggle over the lumps in the road. To bother leaving the house in this town, on these roads, you must have something you really want to do, I thought.

The memorial was empty. Silent but for the invisible birds. A local guide told me of the plans for the memorial, and the history of the place. Both town and tomb. We headed towards the back of the lot, stopping just in front of where the bodies were buried. Everywhere I looked – up to the edges of the woods – were recently upturned patches of yellow soil. Molehills, was my casual assumption. But the guide told me a story. Nobody knew dead Jews lay beneath this land before she and others planned to commemorate the wretched past. Funding found, they made their plaque, built a wall and put up the Star of David, so everyone knew the history that had been hidden. But the problem, she explained, is what else people assumed was buried. Revealing history reveals prejudice too, and, most nights, black market archaeologists return with metal detectors to search for the gold and jewels they guess a Jewish mass grave will hold. In teeth and pockets, as if they would not have been removed by the Nazis in the first place. How tricky all this is. In making people learn about their past, all that has happened so far is the resting have been disturbed and so my thoughts shift back to the present and the Rava-Ruska I have found myself in. How much of a future, really, can a place have when its people are desperate enough to burgle decades-old mass graves? Graves that, given what I knew of my great-grandfather, were probably filled with the bones of my family.

David Schapira was born sixty miles away from Rava Ruska to a family, my family, of 'deeply religious eastern European Jews'. Visits to see them across what read like a startling Galicia – through those 'wide expanse of fields and meadows in flower during spring . . . Glittering snow-covered road and railway tracks in winter . . . The wide expanse of dense pine, broad-leaved forest stretching away in a hilly landscape' – caused him great excitement. Most of all when he went by train to family gatherings through Lviv. It was the biggest town around and, back in his day, before the 1940s, thirty-five synagogues stood in frequently packed use. There is just one now, plus a quiet square in the otherwise gorgeous, bustling, fun, smart, entirely-Christian historical old centre that is only called Synagogue Square because there aren't any synagogues there any more.

I went to Ukraine to find out where I began or rather the site of year zero for what knowledge I have of my family, knowledge which starts with the access granted by David's diaries. Beyond that lies an endlessness of who knows what, people travelling where, back to existences in shacks and homes I guess looking like something out of the northern regions of *Game of Thrones*, but hopefully without the incest.

I have to start somewhere.

My flight to Lviv required a change and three-hour

wait in Warsaw. It would have been quicker to fly via Kiev, but because I'm Western and weak and there was a war near there, in eastern Ukraine, and bombs going off in the capital and a plane that fell from the sky, I opted for a supposedly safer route. As though bombs have never exploded in London, or planes crashed over the Pyrenees. I saw nothing on the flight to Warsaw. It was foggy to begin with, the sky pumped up with clouds. David's memoir sat on my iPad on my lap, and I read it as I listened to a clever pop band sing about modern urban millennial issues with a standout line about posting a photo of salads on the internet. I find that funny. It's my echo chamber within my echo chamber, but as the song ended and clouds broke for my second flight, from Warsaw to Lviv, such flippancy felt a million miles away from the piece of the planet below. Gold glistened on church rooftops in otherwise grey towns, but, every now and then, I'd look closer and take in the pastel shades of the houses below. We landed next to a mural of the flag, blue and yellow faded onto concrete and, for a country supposedly splitting itself in two with war, it was telling how much they boast of their national colours. For a people with such visible national pride, the break-up must be hard; a couple still wearing their wedding rings as they walk to sign their divorce papers.

I spent the night in Lviv. Dinner was chicken, potato cakes, two large beers costing less than a pound each, and memoir-reading. Oleg, I'm told, is turning up at 9.30 in the morning for the drive out to Rava-Ruska. 'I have no real memory of my childhood,' I read, but it's a lie. David's mother died when he was just three and, as his father worked, he describes how he and his two siblings were raised by an aunt, a teenager. His writing lays out major events like a shopping list but becomes fluid, emotional and evocative when talking about the environment in which he was raised. 'We visited the smithy, carpentry, brewery, animal stalls, storage lofts; romped in nearby fields and lanes.' A vast playground for an active boy, who perhaps only had freedom as he had no strong hold over him from anyone or anything else. ('I therefore enjoyed a mother's love and protective security for only the first few years of my childhood.') His father worked from early in the morning until late in the evening, with 'little time or inclination' for the next generation.

At some undefinable point between 1897 and 1914, David's father took a job as a corn merchant in Rava-Ruska. Back then the town was in Poland, not Ukraine, right on the border of the Russian Empire. Ninety per cent orthodox Jewish, moans my ancestor, with the lack of music, theatre and sport which comes with such a level of spiritual service. 'A cinema, and an occasional performance by an amateur theatre group was all that was offered in a very sparse cultural life.' Similar distractions, it seems, appealed to him as they would his son, Heinz, in England later on.

That was life, though, and he got on with it; normal in his teens, detailing his exams ('Good') and finding sociable things to do, such as joining a Polish political movement club called Sokół-Turner, not to make a difference (it lacked leaders, he says), but because it was what young people did.

The building where he met for Sokół-Turner events is still standing, seconds off the main road that runs through Rava-Ruska. It's grand, yellow-painted with a large balcony and small turret up top. It still hosts meetings, some political, some cultural. Opposite is another informational shrine to the town as it was before the Jews were removed. Laminated photos from as far back as 1904, pictures of the outside of the train station taken between 1908 and 1914. Both photos have a boy in them, and it could be David. I know he walked where I stood taking notes about the Sokół-Turner building. He fits those dates, but he wouldn't fit any soon after, he would be long gone. A goodbye to the town only just beginning to remember his name. In his memoir, David writes of the start of summer in 1914. He was seventeen and looking forward to a long holiday that soon he would learn he would need to put on hold.

It's a grey day when I visit, just over a century later, and stand by a place where my great-grandfather used to attend a political club. Suddenly, the shadows lift, as the sun rises and Olha turns cheerily to utter a clearly well-worn phrase.

'In Galicia, everything changes at midday!'

Except, of course, it doesn't. Had David not fled the anti-Semites in 1914, he almost certainly would have been killed by the Nazis in the next world war, and so, oddly, everything bad that happened to him after he left his home town was better than what else could have been.

*

'Heart! Heart! Heart!' Iryna Kotsur has shaped her hands like a heart and is beating that formation against her chest. She loves emotionally-open and elaborate rock music and, despite knowing very little about bands marketed at people decades younger, we are attempting a cross-lingual conversation about Thirty Seconds to Mars and 5 Seconds of Summer. Apparently, according to her friends Volodya Basay and Martha Mogilevska, I look like the lead singer of the former and that makes barriers crumble. They think, my fringe looping under a black beanie, that I must be a superfan. And so I grin. I mean, I'm not. I still have no idea what he looks like, but, luckily, Iryna is also a One Direction fanatic and everybody knows about One Direction. I tell her that my friend Tom has interviewed the band, how he met Harry Styles a couple of times and so, via me, she is three degrees separated from the singer. Her eyes widen. She gasps something I don't understand but is obviously something elated. She beats that heart symbol again and it feels like the time of her young life, now she has met someone who knows someone who has met One Direction. Her Instagram is selfies and painted nails and babies, and there is no salad, sure, but she has taken photos of a lot of polystyrene coffee cups and put them on the internet.

Iryna, Volodya and Martha's secondary school in Rava-Ruska is three storeys of orange, with no indoor toilet. If you need to go, there are two holes in a concrete block outside above a pit of shit. The playground has a couple of football goals and some tyres half-dug into the ground. Downstairs, there is a project on the wall about Tesco. Sheets of A3 and upwards, where students have drawn a building with bright colours and a giant 'Welcome' sign on the roof; ads for 'Fruit. Vegetables. Clothes. Film' on the shop side. On its caption below, it reads, 'If you are traveller in Britain, you know some popular supermarkets: Sainsburys, Tesco, TSB and other'. I don't feel the need to tell them the last one is a bank. They can find out when they come. 'Don't forget,' continues the caption, 'British use "Please" and "Thank you" a lot.'

'Thank you,' I say, nodding, once we're up a narrow staircase and settled in a classroom with old wooden desks, the ones whose work surfaces lift up to hold books. Like all schools I went to in England. Over a dozen Ukrainian greats have portraits lined up above the blackboard, and Olha takes me through them one-by-one. That aside, she's a blast. Mid-fifties, I guess, an ocean of resentment to her government, filling up through a childhood of poverty and rations, Soviet rule, and the years since of barely anything better than what was before, despite the promises of life after the Cold War. The government, she says, think that the biggest problem with the country are its inhabitants, as they want jobs and an end to corruption. It's a Ukrainian joke and they don't mind people leaving, she says, as they send money back. It is the ones with ideas who stay. They are the problem.

Iryna and Volodya are both sixteen, Martha seventeen. We fixed the interview as they are now the age my great-grandfather was when he left the town they call home.

We start with small talk. Iryna was born in Rava-Ruska, and has lived there her entire life. She has left the country, though, travelling in Europe. 'I had chance and I took chance,' she says and speaks enthusiastically of Poland, Italy, a further eighteen countries. Her hair reaches her tummy and her fringe is neat. Jeans and boots, black jumper, she is chatty, confident, the first of the trio to reach forward to greet me, like she thinks this is an opportunity. Volodya is quieter. He was born in the area too, but hasn't left Ukraine. History is his least favourite subject and he is understated; brown high V-neck and jeans; he doesn't say too much, but his points are never wasted, like the other two mumble meaningful verses and he bellows out a catchy chorus. Martha is the most jittery. She smiles a lot but with incredulity. She is not from these parts, but had to flee eastern Ukraine, Donetsk – her home – when war broke out in 2014. Her home city is close to Crimea and rebels who were anti-government and pro-Soviet made life too dangerous. She, too, hasn't yet left her country and says that one day she will return to Donetsk, when it becomes safely Ukrainian again. Her father is still there. He is a volunteer for the army, even though she calls it an unofficial position, whatever that means.

War looms over all sadly phrased questions and hesitant answers. It has to. How can it not? 'This war is not worth any life lost,' says Iryna, via Olha – the former's English is decent but not sufficient, she believes, to tackle what we mostly talk about. 'Nobody needs this war and it is a strange war, and it is difficult to talk about.' Her eyes betray both vulnerability and determination.

'All my life,' says Volodya, having patiently waited his turn, 'I lived in peace and this war is strange. I do not want this war to prolong. I want to stay in Ukraine and help Ukraine, and this war is not understandable for people.' He is resolute, or pragmatic, where Martha is, of course, more directly affected and tells her dramatic story last, with the background of how, in the football championships that took place two years before the war broke out, people chanted how they love Ukraine yet now all the words have changed. They say they have never been from Ukraine. They're Russians. Hate everything Ukrainian and do not want to be from Ukraine.

I tell them about my great-grandfather David and his involvement in Sokół-Turner. 'My early youth,' he writes, 'was influenced by the political tensions before the First World War, which had their precursors in the Balkan wars of 1912–1913 . . . Because I was interested in history I was also interested in political events on a regional and international level, and I eagerly studied reports and read articles in newspapers and magazines about developments in the Balkan wars and their eventual influence and course towards a European war.'

As Olha starts explaining all this to the students, and translates my question to the trio as to whether they are involved in political groups themselves, given the perpetual possibility of war, Martha's mobile rings and it's from *Star Wars*. 'Imperial March', to be precise – the deep and ominous power cry that accompanies tyrant Darth Vader wherever he goes, which seems suitable to what is happening in the east of her country. It's her mum on the line. It was she, her daughter explains, who said they had to flee the east and they came to Rava-Ruska as that is where she was originally from – before moving east. Now much of the east doesn't want her. It's complicated, then. Everyone moves all the time.

Martha watches television with her mother and cries, watching people dying in front of cameras. There are a lot of victims. 'When the war started, me and my mother moved here, having a hope that we will stay here for several weeks and that everything will be OK and everything will finish, but nothing finished,' she says, and she sounds a bit nervous. 'We planned to return, but mother and grandmother were sitting at the television and crying and it seemed no end, no changes. Later, we got tired of news and switched off the TV and if I need some real news I go to my father and he tells me what is really going on in Donetsk, as he stays in Donetsk region, in the Ukrainian part . . .'

Volodya doesn't belong to a political group, but says when the revolution broke out he started to follow the news more and was led to believe everything would be OK, that everything would change.

'But,' he says, 'times passed and people got tired of this news and, recently, my father switches off news as nothing changes and new faces came to power and we had hope, but now it is all the same. All the same corruption . . . No changes and the situation got even worse.'

Iryna is sadder than anyone. Maybe it's because she has seen outside her country and knows what riches and freedom there could be. Eighteen countries in Europe are a lot for a teenager from a small Ukrainian town to have seen. Think about how most British people think about America: wide roads and be anything you want to be – it's so much better over there!

She says she was politically active when the war started in 2014. She would listen to the news and watch television, read newspapers and learn what there was to learn about key actions being taken all over her part of the country. She believed everything would change, but right now, she is disappointed with everything. 'I'm in depression,' she sighs. She doesn't believe the mass media her nation produces, and now fears – or worse, knows – that everything will be as it is for a very long time.

'I was shocked,' she says, 'when I heard the Euro Commission had made a conclusion that Ukraine will not be in European Union for twenty years at least.' She is very sad about this. It looks like she is about to cry, and I decide not to mention the vote the British were set to have about whether we should stay in the Union or not. (We met a couple of months ahead of it.) She wants to study at Oxford University. Law. And her eyes water and she is fed up; sad when she talks of the war in her country. She is devastated by the idea she may have to stay where she is from. I have made only one other person cry in an interview and it was Charlize Theron, over lunch in a Los Angeles members' club. We were talking about South Africa, her home nation, and she started to well up when telling me why she had to leave and how nobody really understands why. She loves that country, but she had a chance to go and to make it and she wishes people understood that. I was left at the table, staring into nothing, as a very famous woman ran off to wipe her eyes. Home, in both cases, is what was able to upset the interviewee the most.

I try to move the conversation onto something more optimistic. Black tea with a bowl of sugar has arrived with at least thirty jam biscuits and, as we sip and nibble, I ask about the internet. Iryna and Martha both have modern smartphones. Volodya leaves his in his pocket, if he has one in the first place. It strikes me as odd that the students all have devices worth at least £200, and yet to go a school with no decent toilet, but such a question would have felt weirdly off-topic.

I look around my table. Two of the teenagers never let their phones out of their hands. Iryna says she communicates with a lot of people on the internet and that it is a 'great possibility' to have 'a wider circle of people than one country'. She says she has a lot of friends all over the world and that 'they're very special . . . very kind and, when they write that we are supporting Ukraine, I say, "I love you!"'

Volodya, meanwhile, says he uses the internet to explore.

'Internet,' he says, 'gives me the idea that I belong to the world, because when I see all countries of the world support Ukraine, I feel I belong to the world.'

So, unlike their parents, and people like their translator Olha, raised under a blanket with everything they were meant to know underneath and everything else above it, Iryna, Volodya and Martha can, theoretically, know it all. So, I ask, do they? If you're unsettled by what you see on the television, is there refuge online? They tell me about VKontakte, a Russian version of Facebook, which is for former Soviet republics and very few foreigners. Before the war, they would all use it regularly and, for that reason, Iryna says the internet is good, and Volodya agrees. He too used VKontakte before the war. But that's where the good news ends; before the war. 'There is a lot of fake in the internet,' says Iryna, sadly. 'And it is possible to write unpleasant things to each other, for example sometimes people came to my page and wrote me very unpleasant things.' She means people who are not on Ukraine's side in the war. 'Their remarks are very aggressive, and I try not to use internet for political purposes. I just communicate with my friends and learn about music news and such.'

'When the war started,' continues Volodya, 'posts were very aggressive and very negative, so that's why I went out of this group and now try to stay in Ukrainian groups, for things like football, but even in football, there is politics and propaganda and I try to avoid Russian posts and Russian contacts because they are like zombie and they write very silly things.'

Then I talk to Martha: 'It is really because the internet is full of fake,' she says, defeated, matter-of-fact, cradling her phone in her hand. 'You can read in the morning, and carry it in your brains for the whole day, and the evening you read that was a joke or not true, and that's why I try to avoid any political information.'

When I ask about history and an interest they may have in what happened to my great-grandfather and the

Jews who stayed too long, they are polite. They care, yes; and a teacher is in the classroom, and they have exams coming up so need to learn – and Martha even talks of Jewish ancestors from Rava-Ruska, who owned a shop that sold products for horses.

But it feels the Jewish memorial and the information board, and recent efforts that remind the current generation of the genocide that ran blood into their soil, is of little interest. When your life is like that of these three teenagers, how can you, really, work yourself up about the local past when everything about your current home is a mess, and the bridges to foreign countries you want to visit are being burnt?

The road out to Stojanow from Rava-Ruska contains at least two patches of rough on which you think strongly about turning back. 'But then why did we come so far?' shouted Oleg, when such an idea was mooted. The suspension in his car was already ruined anyway. We continued, and the closer we got to the town where my great-grandfather David was born the more horse-drawn carriages we saw. Packed with groups of men, tooled up for the farms. The woods and fields, though, were empty. This isn't how he described it in his diary – that read as lush, beautiful – and the only sounds in the town come from the dogs that bark at clucking chickens. There is a café where everybody seems to be loitering. A smooth stone statue salutes the war dead. It's shaped like a crouching soldier. I wander off to a corrugated iron bus stop. It is empty. Just ads from people flogging services and the furniture they don't need.

A full timetable handwritten in black ink catches my eye. Most of the time, there is one bus an hour and the buses, unlike any I've ever seen, are like a normal single-decker cut in half lengthways. It can't fit more than thirty and routes are very long. A bin by the stop has been crashed into. It remains dented like a creased-up map.

Back in Rava-Ruska, in the classroom over biscuits, with their teacher near, for whom it was too late to change anything about her life, I asked my teenagers if they planned to stay in Ukraine. Martha was torn. She wants to be an illustrator for children's books and knows that there are more opportunities to study and work abroad. But she would like to return, hopefully to where she is actually from, where there is, right now, a war. It is where she thinks she belongs.

Her friend Iryna, though, is leaving. 'So,' she explains, not sounding at all excited, but rather deeply practical, 'now I see our country goes back and becomes more and more backward, because of corruption, that is why, in my sixteen years I have already made my decision and my parents support me. I will move abroad. I want to live a normal life and I always will love Ukraine and am ready to return any moment, but I want to live normal life. My dream is to become a student of university abroad and to learn law. But I have to improve my skills.'

Volodya, as ever, says less. His opportunities seem narrower. 'For me,' he says, 'I will stay in Ukraine as somebody must stay in the country and change the country, and I have no opportunity to go abroad and enter university. So I decided to stay and I have hope we'll unite our efforts and change something for the best.'

In a small wooden church in Stojanow, Olha talked to the congregation about the party she was with. This group of British people asking a lot of questions, taking photos, being hugely respectful. A woman told her about a Jewish cemetery in their town that was over a hundred years old. Take a left, then a left, past a pretty blue wooden house that dates back to the beginning of the last century, up a bad road. You can't miss it.

The gate that opens on five stones standing up like obelisks is painted in yellow and decorated with many small stars of David. None of us there speaks Hebrew, so inscriptions remain unknown but the mind will wander. We know that my great-great grandmother Amalia – who died when her son David was three – passed away in Stojanow and never made it to Rava-Ruska. She was, of course, Jewish, so she must be buried here. It is and always has been the only Jewish cemetery in town.

My mum takes a stone and places it gently on the grave. She remains stoic, like her foreign father would have, because they are British and so don't like to be emotional in public. There are no tears then, but it's not just because of who she is as a person. She knows she has been lucky too. Whatever happened, after these ancestors of ours ended their association with Ukraine, or Poland, as it was, only helped us in our own lives. Giving us the sort of opportunity that the British take for granted and which, across the full spectrum of society, makes some believe they have the right to keep to themselves. They say, after all, that there is no more room.

How could we possibly take any people in?

It's tricky writing a book about an old topic that won't go away. Every day, often to your surprise and depression, something happens that means all of yesterday's work is outdated. Who would have thought, for instance, only a couple of years ago, that the President of the United States would start threatening to publish lists of crimes caused by immigrants? If I had published this five years ago, when the far-right was less prominent and nobody needed to ask about the ethics of punching a Nazi, the tone would have been cautiously optimistic. A world full of leaders my great-grandfather would have been impressed by. Now, the tone is desperately trying not to be defeatist. One day, I read a convincing argument, backed up with graphs and pie charts, which suggested that the vote for Brexit and the horrid conservatism of Donald Trump are not signs of a new trend, but the dying embers of an old generation – their last chance at control in a world they are rapidly losing. That sounds nice, but the people at rallies all over the world for extremist politics are hardly all geriatric. This is not a generational malaise and so, yes, one day I read something that makes me feel OK, but the next, someone passes a bill to appease the racists in their country – and it's back to disbelief again.

Maybe the only conclusion is confusion. Amazingly, some British citizens, post-Brexit, looked to Jewish ancestors from Germany and Austria, who had come here during the war, and tried to reclaim their family's lost nationality in an attempt to stay European. What an irony. A country that people fled to because it was tolerant and safe has become a place many don't feel welcome in and, therefore, they want to go back.

I could, I guess, look into an Austrian passport, as they are members of the EU. The mountains are beautiful and Vienna is yet to have a major terrorist incident. But then I remember Adham's fear and that country's recent elections and realise that working out where you belong takes a lot longer than it used to.

Title Note

There is a song by the American songwriter Conor Oberst, writing under his Bright Eyes pseudonym, called 'I Must Belong Somewhere'. Oberst is my favourite songwriter. A man who put eccentric prose into beautiful songs and protested loudly against George W. Bush, 'I Must Belong Somewhere' is bouncy and upbeat. Many verses focus on things staying where they are ('Leave the garden tools in the rusted shed / Leave those bad ideas in your troubled head today'), leading to the rousing chorus of 'Everything – it must belong somewhere'. He sounds tired but self-sufficient. 'I couldn't catch my breath,' Oberst said at the time, about writing the song. 'I calmed down by listing everything that I could think of and its place in the world. Not where I designed it to be – but where it is . . . [It's] the idea that sometimes you have to sit still . . . be where you are, regardless of any expectations, things people want you to do. It's about being content in your own skin.'

I thought the name of the song would be a good title for this book.